PRIMITIVE LAW

PRIMITIVE LAW

BY

E. SIDNEY HARTLAND, F.S.A.

KENNIKAT PRESS
Port Washington, N. Y./London

PRIMITIVE LAW

First published in 1924
Reissued in 1970 by Kennikat Press
Library of Congress Catalog Card No: 79-115320
ISBN 0-8046-1111-4

Manufactured by Taylor Publishing Company   Dallas, Texas

CONTENTS

PRIMITIVE LAW

CHAPTER I

INTRODUCTORY

MAN is a social being. He is never found alone, save under the compulsion of exceptional and temporary circumstances. In this he differs from the higher apes, his nearest analogues in nature, which are usually solitary or found at most in tiny bands consisting of an adult male, his female consort, and their immature progeny. Human beings, on the contrary, if they separate in the search for food, flight from enemies, or other purposes, always rejoin the band to which they belong at the earliest opportunity ; and where, as frequently among the lowest races, they habitually gather in small companies, these coalesce either at stated times, or on summons for consultation touching matters of common interest, for the performance of common rites, or for other social purposes. Such aggregates, whether of few or many, whether temporary or permanent, necessitate rules governing the relations of the individuals composing them to one another and to the aggregate, and the relations of the aggregate and of individuals composing it to similar

aggregates and to alien individuals in general. Without these rules the assembly or the band would be a
mere agglomeration of individuals guided only by their
individual wills : it could not continue to exist.

Such governing rules are the laws which the individuals and aggregates alike obey. In the lower
culture—that is to say, among relatively primitive
peoples—these laws are to the present day unwritten ;
and presumably this was the case universally in archaic
times. Hence, among civilized peoples who are
accustomed to associate laws with written documents,
the rules obeyed by savage peoples have been refused
the name of laws and called only customs. But customs
that are fixed and generally obeyed are indistinguishable from laws. In our own country, the judges of
the King's courts have always recognized and given
effect to them as laws, though prescribed in no written
legislation. Thus modes of action and conduct which
have been followed from time immemorial by the
community, or by particular classes or districts, as
definite and proper rules for the guidance of transactions, or of the relations between different sections
of the community or between individuals, have been
stamped with general approval and become part of
express law. On the same authority the resentment and
repudiation by the community, without any formal
prohibition by the sovereign, of conduct defined as
contra bonos mores have been adopted, and this conduct
has been declared contrary to the public interest and
good government. Both on the positive and the
negative sides custom has been recognized as law.

The first attempt at codifying Roman law was the
Law of the Twelve Tables, assigned to the year 450 B.C.

But nobody suggests that unwritten, but real, laws did not exist long prior to this. Rome had then been an independent and growing State for ages. Indeed, we expressly hear of new laws and changes of law long before the promulgation of the Law of the Twelve Tables. Our own forefathers, the English of the period called the Heptarchy, had no written laws until after the coming of Christianity at the end of the sixth century. The earliest written legislation by the kings and their witan that has come down to us is obviously nothing more than a series of attempts to supplement and adapt to the new order of things a body of law already of ancient date. Kent was naturally the first kingdom to do so ; and the new laws of Kent in more than one instance speak of their kings as thus adding to the laws of the forefathers. The legislation of Ina, King of the West Saxons, also presupposes the existence of a body of laws, which it is intended to supplement and amend. It is needless to labour the point.

In these pages we have only to do with Primitive Law, the rules which govern societies in the lower culture. The word *primitive* must not be taken literally. We do not know what laws governed mankind in an absolutely primitive condition. No records remain of that condition when human beings first emerged as such—when men first became men. Of their societies, therefore, we know nothing. We can only infer that mankind must have been evolved from gregarious ancestors. The process was doubtless slow and extremely gradual ; and the co-operation of numbers was a material element in bringing about the result. Co-operation implies a certain degree of harmony ;

and the harmony must have been attained by some kind of rudimentary regulation. That such regulation was possible the examples of deer and even bees and ants, which have not risen above the merely animal condition, abundantly prove. Much more, then, was it natural to creatures endowed with higher capacities, and hence with greater possibilities of advance. Our acquaintance with human societies begins at a much later date. The most backward societies of men now are at least societies of men with human needs, human feelings, and human aspirations. It is to these, and to societies somewhat more advanced, that anthropologists apply the term *primitive*. Its use is necessarily comparative and vague, as many terms are which relate to the subjects or the consequences of Evolution.

The laws of all such societies are unwritten, because writing is unknown ; or, if it be known, not in common use. But the laws themselves are well known. In England, in consequence of the growing complexity of civilization, the presumption everywhere underlying legal administration, that every one knows the law, has ceased for generations to correspond with the facts, and has been expressly limited by the courts of law so as to exclude the operation of certain details of the law of property. In a simpler society, the difficulty cannot arise. From his earliest days the everyday life of the tribe is exposed to the child. He becomes acquainted with the meaning of his surroundings, the occupations and duties of the individuals composing the tribe, its divisions and organization, as they are revealed in the acts and in the talk of all about him. At the age of puberty, when his understanding has sufficiently ripened with his years, he is brought together with his fellows of similar age under a more formal and penetrating discipline, in the course of which he is initiated into the secret tribal traditions and ideals and the rules which are to guide his life as an adult member of the community. Thenceforth in constant communion with the elders he profits by their knowledge and experience, until his memory is stored and his judgment is matured on all the questions of tribal as well as sectional and individual rights and duties. Such a result is possible only where the community is comparatively small, and where its civilization is rudimentary and uncomplicated by the division of labour, the machinery, the accumulation of property, the ranks and social divisions of more advanced societies.

Primitive law—the law of societies we call primitive— relates of course to rude conditions, in which culture has made but little progress, and in which the more elemental conditions demand little of the elaboration rendered ever more and more necessary by expanding civilization. On the other hand, it covers whole departments of life that we have abandoned to the unfettered will of the individual, or at all events dropped from the law of which cognizance is taken by the courts of justice. Many of these, it is true, are still governed by our social customs, or by the rules of voluntary societies within the body politic ; but they are matters which do not affect foreign relations, the King's peace within the realm, the descent of property, the conditions of labour, taxation, or other subjects to which in modern days we confine the enactment and administration of what is with us technically the law. Primitive law is in truth the totality of the customs of the tribe. Scarcely anything eludes its grasp. The savage lives more in public than we do ; any deviation from the ordinary mode of conduct is noted, and is visited with the reprobation of one's fellows. It is a common thing to ascribe any untoward event which may happen afterwards to such a deviation.[1] A man's relations with his mother-in-law are a subject for jocularity with us ; the community does not interest itself seriously in them, unless he transgress the etiquette of the position with the kitchen poker. It is otherwise with the Blackfellows of Australia. Among the Yuin of New South Wales a man might not even look at his mother-in-law ; and even if his shadow fell on her it was a cause of divorce. The tribes on the Hunter River, at the mouth of which the thriving port of Newcastle now stands, were more severe : to do no more than speak to her was death.[2]

It is a serious offence against the law of the Ifugao of Northern Luzon in the Philippine Islands to use certain language or do certain acts in the presence of one's kin of the opposite sex who are within the prohibited degrees of marriage, or indeed to refer to sexual matters save in the most delicately veiled manner. Breach of the taboo was generally punished by social contempt ; but in one district it rendered the culprit liable to be punished by the lance, especially if a third

[1] An instance may be given of the effect of deviation in what we should think a very trifling matter. Among the Bantu of South Africa " a man must never sleep on the right-hand side of the bed when he occupies the same bed with one of his wives. He must not touch her with his right hand ; *if he did he would have no strength in war, and would surely be slain.*"—Rev. J Macdonald in " J. A. I.," XX, 140.

[2] Howitt, 266, 267.

person were present. No one among the same people
who knows of a death may ask a relative of the dead
man if he be dead ; he who does so is punishable by
fine.[1] At a death among the Arunta of Central Australia it is the duty of all the actual and (under Arunta
law) possible sons-in-law of the deceased to cut themselves on the shoulder ; and to omit to do so is to render
the offender liable to punishment at the hands of some
other father-in-law, actual or possible, by forfeiture of
his wife, who will be given away to another man.[2]
Their northern neighbours, the Warramunga, forbid
certain foods, including the flesh of a kind of kangaroo
(*Macropus robustus*), to all except very old men, and
for anyone else to eat this kind of kangaroo is a grave
offence.[3] Among the Ewhe of the Slave Coast of West
Africa " the most absolute tolerance prevails with
regard to the worship of the gods, and it is considered
quite natural that opinions should differ concerning
the choice of a god. Sacrileges or insults to a god,
however, are always resented and punished by the
priests and worshippers of that god, it being their duty
to guard his honour." [4] Do we pity or despise these poor
savages and barbarians for the importance they attach
to such trifles ? In the fifteenth and sixteenth centuries, on a much higher plane of civilization, we burnt
alive, by sentence of the courts, men and women for the
crime of heresy, and we compelled every one to attend
his own parish church every Sunday and ecclesiastical

[1] R. F. Barton, " Univ. Cal. Pub.," XV, 12.
[2] Spencer and Gillen, " Central Tribes," 500 ; " Northern
Tribes," 514, 515.
[3] *Ibid.*, " Northern Tribes," 515.
[4] [Sir] A. B. Ellis, " Ewe," 81.

holiday—a law which was only repealed in the tenth year of the late Queen Victoria, within the lives of many persons yet surviving.

Some of these prohibitions and injunctions raise the question of the sanction necessary to a law. The subject will be considered more at large hereafter. In the meanwhile it is enough to observe that social contempt often carries very real penalties in the lower culture; and even supernatural penalties, the vengeance of a god or the self-acting power of a taboo, are the creation of society. The general belief in the certainty of supernatural punishment and the alienation of the sympathy of one's fellows generate an atmosphere of terror which is quite sufficient to prevent a breach of tribal customs, such as would be held to account for a personal or tribal calamity.

Tribal law does not recognize the divisions which are found convenient in juridical discussions. The law is one; every part of it is equally consecrated by long use, by religion, and by the instinctive submission of every member of the tribe. In these stages of culture, in the same way as the name is an essential part of the individual, the law is an essential part of the tribe. It is no question of aim or utility. Every portion of it is equally binding and has the same reputed origin; every portion equally belongs to the traditions of the tribe and is a sacred inheritance from the tribal ancestors. The law is a manifestation of the tribal life, as indivisible as life itself. This is not to say that there is no change, no legislation.

No one will venture to affirm that any community has remained perfectly stationary during the centuries or millenniums that have elapsed from its beginning, whatever that beginning may have been. There has been constant change, usually very slow and gradual, and then for the most part unconscious, but at times sudden or greatly accelerated. Contact with other communities, with other civilizations, with new and unfamiliar physical environments, is among its most obvious causes. Internal expansion, too, has led to continual developments ; for apart from outside influences the growth and evolution of a living organism have been acting throughout its existence. But the new law rests on the old foundation and speedily becomes consolidated with it. For scientific purposes, therefore, while we analyse Primitive Law into different subjects, in the hope of rendering it more intelligible, it must be always borne in mind that the " primitive " does not so analyse it. He accepts it as a whole, a unity, the thought of analysing which has never entered his head.

CHAPTER II

CONSTITUTIONAL LAW

THE first requisite of every community is to have some sort of organization which provides for the seat of authority, the method and extent of its exercise, and the internal arrangements governing the relations of its various parts. This is the constitution of the society. In communities the most nearly primitive of any now existing the constitution is of the most elementary kind. The organization depends in the first place upon the food-supply and the means of obtaining food, and next upon the foes, human and other, with whom the community has to contend. Some of the peoples in this condition inhabit the most remote and inhospitable regions of the earth's surface. They have probably been driven thither by the pressure of tribes better equipped and more vigorous than themselves. In this case they may have reached in the happier seats from which they have been driven a higher zone of civilization than they now occupy ; and they may have been compelled to abandon culture and organization unsuited to their present habitat and condition. But although this is possible there is little or no evidence of such degradation. So far as we know, it may be said generally that peoples in such a situation show no signs of having once been more civilized than they are to-day. They may therefore be taken as exhibiting an early type of society. Other peoples in a low condition of culture dwelling in a land more favoured with the means for human habitation and progress have an elementary constitution in many respects not a whit more advanced than theirs.

The archipelago which we call collectively Tierra del Fuego is inhabited by several tribes, of which little is scientifically known. The Yahgan are the most southerly of these tribes. They inhabit the desolate shores of the Beagle Channel and the equally desolate islands southward to Cape Horn. They seem to have no tradition of ever having lived anywhere else. In their bitterly cold and stormy environment the Yahgans are naked savages, having at most a sealskin or a sea-otter skin thrown over their shoulders to protect them in some measure from the driving gales and icy waters, amid which they contrive to preserve a miserable existence. In those chilly regions where little vegetable life can be maintained, they extract nourishment from a few funguses, berries and roots, but chiefly depend on the produce of the sea—fish, seals, molluscs, and now and then stranded whales—and on the eggs of sea-birds. This precarious life has chiefly to be passed in canoes, each of which represents an independent authority, containing for the most part only a family group, commanded by the father or the most experienced and able seaman. Ashore they are housed in rough wigwams, in which a family or two may dwell. At times they assemble in larger numbers at a fixed rendezvous, where they may remain for weeks, dividing socialistically the plunder of the seas, or whatever else chance may have thrown in their way. But the duration of these assemblies is precarious ; the necessities of life and the uncontrolled will of the chief of a family group may bring it at any time to an end. It follows from what has been said that the only fixed authority recognized is that of a father over his family ; there are no other chiefs, though an influence, real but undefined, is exercised by experience and proved strength, intelligence, and ability, or by the medicine-man's craft and skill in his management of men. A father's power over his wife or wives and other dependants is in theory absolute ; in practice it is greatly limited by the power and independence of the women. There is, however, no social inequality, neither slavery nor aristocracy being recognized. Definite clan-organization does not exist, but the germs of it may perhaps be found in the fact that certain groups " related apparently by blood and marriage occupy more or less fixed localities."

The tribal constitution is here in a distinctly rudimentary stage. No other is possible in the cruel environment. Yet we are told that " the Yahgan is as gregarious as his food-supply and *wanderlust*, the latter if not engendered at least nursed by his habitat, will permit," and that " only lack of greater communal intercourse is responsible for lack of leaders." [1]

In the stormy Bay of Bengal the inhabitants of the Andaman Islands, a negrito people, are very low in the scale of humanity. They are acquainted with the use of fire, but do not know how to produce it. They are divided into a number of independent tribes, among

[1] Proc. 19th Internat. Cong. Americanists, 426 *sqq.* ; " Bull. B. E.," LXIII, 168, 177, 188-199, 225.

which the entire country is apportioned. The climate is tropical, the islands are covered more or less with jungle, and life is less arduous than that of the Yahgans ; larger communities are therefore possible. Roots, fruits and seeds of various kinds, honey, shellfish, fish, and turtle on the sea-shore, inland the produce of the chase, such as mammals, iguanas, snakes, and certain insects, constitute the main food-supply, occasionally varied with pigeons or jungle-fowls. To obtain these they have to live a nomadic life, each tribe and each local group within its own limits. They dwell in huts, more or less fragile according as they are intended for a comparatively permanent camp or to serve only temporary ends. There is no organized government, nor any chiefs properly so called. The persons who have been called chiefs in the writings of Mr. Man, and even of Sir R. C. Temple, appear to be in fact no more than men whose personal qualities of skill in hunting and fishing, their boldness and enterprise in war, and their reputation for generosity, hospitality, and evenness of temper have led them to eminence among the older men. It is the older men and women who manage the affairs of the community and get the best share of the good things of Andamanese life. Each tribe consists of a number of independent local groups or communities, united only by a common language and such common feeling as it generates with neighbours who are known, and who are known to be on the whole friendly and to have certain common interests. In themselves the local groups are but loosely bound to-gether : a member who is discontented can always quit his group and join another which may be willing to receive him. In the management of affairs the elders are therefore subject to the will of the group ; and, if in the distribution of food and other matters they get any personal advantage, it is because this is conceded to their known qualities and experience and to the tradition of the community. Moreover, younger men attach themselves willingly to elders of known ability, and increase their following and their local group. There is no distinction of rank or class: apart from age and personal character all are on equal terms. But there is a further division of the people into long-shore men and jungle-dwellers, according to their respective habitat and habits, each of these divisions in each tribe having its own elders and leaders.[1]

The constitution of the Andamanese tribe, accordingly, is still founded on voluntary association and obedience. If it be any higher than that of the Yahgans, it owes it to the larger and more permanent aggregations of individuals composing it, and consequently a greater and more continuous common feeling and co-operation. The people are not separated by the need of seeking food on barren islets and on the seas, where numbers would be of little avail and could not be supplied with the requisites of life. They dwell in the jungle, or on shores that furnish them with more liberal supplies. On the other hand, co-operation is needed for the erec-tion of their comparatively permanent encampments, for the hunt, and for protection against neighbouring tribes, some of which are warlike and addicted to raids across the frontiers of their respective territories. Assistance is willingly given, for the sustenance and

---

[1] E. H. Man, " J. A. I.," XII, 108 ; Sir R. C. Temple, " Census of India, 1901," 49, 51. Both the accounts have been much modified by subsequent inquiries.

often the very existence of the local community and the tribe are at stake. It should also not be forgotten that the association and obedience of the individual members may be voluntary only in appearance and in detail. The habit is impressed on them from their earliest years. It becomes part of their character. They cannot imagine any other mode of existence ; and to act contrary to the customs of the tribe or the wishes of the elders would be to challenge public opinion and to render them outcasts, unless in a particular case they had strong grounds for their action and the sympathy of a considerable proportion of their fellows.

In a similar zone of civilization the Australian tribe differs in organization from that of the negritoes of the Andaman Islands in several respects. As in the case of the latter, each tribe occupies and hunts over a certain territory whose limits, however ill-defined they may seem to us, are well understood by the natives. The tribe within those limits speaks a common language and recognizes a certain kind of kinship uniting all its members ; but it has no chief, nor any large permanent community. The quest of food divides it into small parties, sometimes consisting of no more than a Yahgan boatload—an adult man with his wives and children—at other times of a greater number, but usually all related by blood or marriage, roving about within a certain area over which they have a special claim, and camping together in miserable temporary huts, or often under the shelter of mere wind-screens. These small parties are, however, more or less in touch with neighbouring parties, and with them form what may be termed a local group, which meets now and then for ceremonial functions, consultations, hunting, and social amuse-

ment. More rarely the entire tribe assembles for these
purposes, and less frequently still two or more tribes
speaking dialects of a common language.[1] Such
meetings, if food can be ensured, may be prolonged over
days and even weeks ; but the conditions forbid anything more than an occasional reunion. The strongest
tie between the units of a tribe is perhaps that of
language, which gives substance to the vague feeling
of kinship between the different local groups. Each
local group, whether large or small, is very jealous of
any violation of what is deemed its special territory, and
such violation may, and frequently does, lead to war.[2]
Although the tribe has no single chief whose power is
recognized by all the units, there is as a rule one man in
each local group who takes an undefined leadership and
from his ability and experience is recognized in that
capacity. On his death he is often succeeded by his
son, if qualified in the same way. Such a man wields
in his local group much influence. His authority is
rarely set at defiance ; but it is indefinite, and is armed
with no compelling power. Beyond the limits of the
local group he comes into competition with other local
leaders. Both in the local group and in the tribe the
real power is vested in the old men, who form a sort of
council whose decisions are generally accepted ; and
of this council the local leaders (often called the headmen) naturally form part. The constitution of the
council, however, is vague, and its decisions, when

---

[1] It is convenient to refer chiefly to G. C. Wheeler, " The
Tribe," because he has analysed the frequently vague and even
contradictory reports of observers who are first-hand authorities.
" The Tribe," 18, 20, 28, 62, 76 ; Howitt, 41.

[2] Wheeler, 41 *sqq.*

made known, are subject to the acquiescence of the general body.[1]

Another division cuts across those of the local group and the tribe, namely, the clan. Save among certain tribes every native belongs to a clan, theoretically a body of blood-relatives into which he is born. This body transcends the local group and the tribe. Indeed, so wide are its ramifications that it is probably not too much to say that many of the clans, or clans which are held to be their equivalents, are found from one end of the continent to the other. We shall consider the clan more in detail hereafter. Meanwhile it is sufficient to observe that the claim to blood-kinship is not the vague kinship of the tribe, but a definite relation founded on descent on one side, and on one side only, either through the mother, as seems to have been the original reckoning, or through the father, which is now the reckoning of some of the tribes. Among the Central tribes the clans are in process of disappearing. The Arunta have already practically discarded them in favour of local groups, centred round the shrines of perpetually reincarnated ancestors. At the head of each of such local groups is a leader who is believed to be a reincarnation of one of the ancestors, and the group over which he in some sense rules bears the name of the clan the shrine of whose previous incarnations it is believed to be in possession of. The local group continues the reincarnation of the dead, and is recruited not by descent but by children who are believed to be reincarnations because their mothers are held to have conceived not by sexual coition, but by the

[1] Wheeler, 49 *sqq.*

entry in some mysterious way into their wombs of the spirits of the deceased.[1]

The clan is exogamous, that is to say, no member is allowed to marry another of the same clan, for this is held to be incest.[2] A further development in organization has, however, taken place almost all over Australia, by which the tribe is divided into marriage-classes. These marriage-classes seem to have been developed out of the clan-system. In the tribes of simplest organization they coincide with the clans. In this case there are only two marriage-classes, which results in dividing the clans into two phratries; and marriages are only permitted between members of opposite phratries.[3] This, however, does not of itself prevent marriages of very near kin. If the rule of descent were matrilineal, for instance, it would not prevent the marriage of father and daughter, for they would belong to opposite phratries; if patrilineal, it would not prevent the marriage of a son with his mother. The next step therefore is to divide the marriage-class into two. Every member of a marriage-class belongs to one or other of these divisions or secondary classes, and the children of a marriage belong to the class of the parent of the sex through whom descent is reckoned, but to the secondary or sub-class to which the parent does not belong. Most of the tribes having the original marriage-classes only, or the original marriage-classes and the secondary classes, reckon descent through the mother only. Some of the Central tribes have still

[1] Spencer and Gillen, "Central Tribes," Chap. IV.
[2] Howitt, 176, 189, 203, etc; Spencer and Gillen, "Central Tribes," 60; Frazer, "Totemism," I, 53.
[3] Howitt, 175; Spencer and Gillen, "Central Tribes," 60.

further developed the system by sub-dividing the secondary classes, each into two tertiary classes. All these tribes reckon descent through the father. His children belong to his primary and secondary classes, but not to his tertiary class. They are assigned to a tertiary class to which he does not belong, and his grandchildren to another tertiary class, with neither of which can he intermarry. The whole tribe is thus divided into eight sub-classes, into only one of which is any member allowed to marry. This artificial arrangement seems to have been devised to prevent the marriage of near kin among a scanty population in which the choice of a spouse was already not too wide, and in which the negotiation of a marriage was a matter of high import to the community.[1] This at least is its effect ; but it also prevents the intermarriage of many persons who, as we reckon kin, are in no way related to each other. In a low stage of culture, however, kinship is reckoned on what is called the classificatory system, which appears to have in view the relation not of individuals to one another, but of classes. Thus the father and all his brothers, as well as certain of those whom we call cousins and others of the same generation outside the lines of what we esteem as kindred, are reckoned as fathers, the mother and all her sisters, together with certain cousins, as we reckon them, and other women of the same generation, as mothers, and so on. It is not that the " primitive " does not know who is his real mother, or does not recognize his mother's husband as his real father, but the actual mother or father is one of a class all of whom sustain for purposes

[1] Howitt, 199 *sqq.* ; Frazer, " Totemism," I, 60 *sqq*, IV, 105 *sqq.*; Roth, 56, 69.

of social order a certain relationship to him. As the sense of dependence and affection develop among persons brought into close and continuous contact, the feeling of kindred becomes more and more individual and acute, and the marriage regulations, unless sufficiently systematized by such a device as the Australian marriage-classes, overflow in supplementary prohibitions, similar in principle to those in use in civilized countries; the clan tends to die away and be superseded as an active institution by the family.

The constitution of the Australian tribe thus exhibits a higher capacity for organization than is exhibited either in the Yahgan or in the Andamanese tribe. It is true that the permanent aggregation of any large number of individuals into a community is rendered impossible by their surroundings and their low civilization; there are no tribal chiefs and no ranks of society; all men are equal, save so far as their personal character may raise them in the estimation of their local group to some kind of leadership. The clans, however, bind together the units of society into an association by what are believed to be ties of blood; and on these are superimposed the marriage-classes as a further step in organization, very useful in default of any distinction such as is in a higher society found in the different ranks and occupations.

The isolation of the Australian Blackfellows for immemorial ages, like that of the peoples previously considered, has doubtless resulted in the perpetuation of their rudimentary civilization and the continuance of the democratic constitution of the tribe. Had they been subjected to invasion by other peoples they must have been dispossessed of the continent, or a great part of it, and ultimately annihilated, or they must have been conquered by and intermingled with them, so as to form a people with institutions of a much more elaborate character. The same cause has preserved, on a much higher level of civilization, a condition of society in many respects comparable with that of the Andamanese and the Australian natives. The Philippine Islands have a population of Malay origin, composed of a number of tribes in various stages of culture. Those inhabiting the lowlands have suffered the domination of Mohammedan conquerors, and after them of the Spaniards, who have brought in various religious and social customs, as well as more material elements of culture. But the mountaineers, by virtue of their greater inaccessibility, have retained their independence, and with it more primitive institutions. Since the Americans have been masters of the islands they have penetrated where the Spaniards never succeeded in going ; and several of the interior tribes have been carefully and scientifically studied. Of these the Ifugao, inhabiting a mountain region in the centre of the northern part of the Island of Luzon, present with many advanced features a very archaic social and political type. They are agriculturists, whose staple industry—putting aside the gentle art of head-hunting, now suffering eclipse by reason of American persistence in rendering the practice uncomfortable—is the growth of rice, supplemented by that of sweet potatoes and some other vegetables of less importance. Upon rice they chiefly depend for their subsistence. For its cultivation they have carved their steep mountain-sides into terraces with wooden spades and wooden crowbars. Many of these terraces are walled with stone, and some of them

are as much as fifty feet high.   All of them are irrigated
with the water from their mountain-streams.   " Without his knowing it," we are told, the Ifugao " bases his
agriculture on scientific principles (to an extent that
astounds the white man) ; and he tends his crops so
skilfully and artistically that he probably has no peer
as a mountain husbandman." [1]

Yet the same authority goes on to declare that " of
political organization the Ifugao has nothing—not
even a suggestion. Notwithstanding, he has a well-
developed system of laws."   There is no central
authority, but the law rests on the unit of the family.
" The mutual duty of kinsfolk and relatives, each
individual to every other of the family, regardless of
sex, is to aid, advise, assist, and support in all controversies and altercations with members of other groups
or families."   " The family is a little democracy in which
each individual is measured for what he is worth, and
has a value accordingly in the family policy."   It is
" an executive and judicial body. Its councils are
informal, but its decisions are none the less effective."
Consequently, the first principle of Ifugao jurisprudence
is that the family solidarity is to be preserved.   It is the
family that punishes offences against itself or against
individual members ; for every offence against an
individual member is an offence against the whole
family.   The Ifugaos are divided geographically into
districts and villages.   But disputes do not take place
between these : only between families ; and peace is
made between families.   " But peace between the
principal families of two villages or districts was some-

[1] R. F. Barton, " Univ. Cal. Pub." XV, 9.

times in effect a peace between the districts or villages involved," though it may have been uncertain and not to be depended on. War between families and the punishment of offences were conducted by a well-understood procedure, which we shall consider here-after.[1]

In fact, the family is the only organization known to Ifugao law. As such, it plays a large part in Ifugao life : it is responsible for the acts and defaults of all its members ; it is capable of holding property in the shape of lands, water rights, and valuable portable articles deemed to be heirlooms, which can only be alienated in cases of extreme necessity and with the consent of the kin, registered by solemn ceremonies. In the face of all this it is odd that the term " family " is never defined by the only investigator whose account has been published. As far as we can gather, it consists of all the relatives, paternal and maternal, by blood or marriage, within vague limits, of any given person. It is not the same for any two persons unless they are brothers or sisters of the whole blood and unmarried. By marriage a man or woman acquires new relations—the relations of the spouse ; and they continue to form part of his or her family, though with a lighter tie than blood-relations, so long as the marriage subsists. This shifting·nature of the family introduces an enormous complexity into Ifugao society. Since the rights and liabilities involved are so extensive, a marriage is usually arranged for children at an early age. When entered into by adults it is commonly preceded by an informal " trial " marriage. A permanent marriage is entered

---

[1] Barton, 15, 92, 109.

into with the consent of the families on both sides, testified by repeated festivities, and including an assignment, somewhat resembling in effect what is called in English law a settlement, to the children of the property they are intended to inherit.[1]

A similar society, but even more peaceable, is that of the Eskimo. The peace of Ifugao society is, or used to be, broken from time to time by head-hunting, which naturally occasioned family feuds. The Eskimo on the Arctic shores of North America and north-eastern Asia had not this source of quarrel to add to such disputes as inevitably arise in a human community. Distributed along the coasts for thousands of miles from east to west, their customs vary in detail, and are partly dependent upon their immediate surroundings. They are, however, in general agreement. In winter the Eskimo are congregated together in snow huts, or huts built of rough stones and drift-wood, and they are supported by the labour and daring of the men in fishing for seals in skin-covered kayaks on the tempestuous seas. The unit of society is a family consisting normally of husband, who is the protector, provider, and ruler, his wife or wives, and children. More than one family sometimes lives in a hut, and the huts are collected in little settlements, each comprising several huts. There is no chief, nor any clan. The sole divisions are the family as above defined, and beyond this the housemates, and in a settlement containing more than one hut the placemates. A vague feeling of comradeship is engendered by dependence on the labours and adventures of the men ; and their produce

---

[1] Barton, 17, 18, 19, 29 n., 39, 40, 92.

is divided first among the family primarily dependent on them. If it be larger than suffices for the family it is shared with the housemates and the placemates. Every community is governed by its public opinion. No one ventures, as a rule, to run counter to the public sentiment or the customs of the tribe, which are well known. What happens when anyone does so we shall consider in another chapter.

When the long and bitter winter passes away the community scatters, and its organization, such as it is, disappears until the winter and darkness return. The families on the mainland go to dwell for a while in tents. The men hunt the seal and walrus, they fish for salmon in the now ice-free streams, they hunt the various land animals of which they can make use as food ; the women gather such berries and other vegetables and small animals as the climate affords. Sometimes small parties set out in kayaks, visiting others, or hunting on land or sea in a comparatively distant area, returning with winter to their own settlement when it reassembles, or settling down elsewhere. There is nothing to compel them to come back, except their own choice, motived by usage and affection for their own wives, parents, or children, or friendship with their old placemates. The whole settlement often removes to another location for good reason approved by the community. Or it may divide if it be difficult to live peaceably together, or if a sufficient body of members prefer another site.[1]

Although not held together so strictly by the family

[1] Nansen, 104, 108, 119 ; Rink, 23, 26, 31 ; " R. B. E.," VI, 576 *sqq.* (cf. Mauss, " L'Année Soc.," IX, 39 *sqq.*) ; " R. B. E.," IX, 427.

organization as the Ifugao, nor limited as the latter are by the immediate contiguity of other tribes, and although more adventurous and more given to wander than they, the Eskimo are not without bonds. They may be born in a community or settlement, and they may be retained in it by sentiment or by ties of relationship, or they may join by their own free will; but they know that once in a community they must act in accordance with the common opinion, and their manner of life must be regulated by the immemorial customs from which they cannot escape, even by joining another. Every member of a community has a voice in its decisions; and hardly even the shaman has a privileged position. But much deference is shown to elders.

We have now considered some typical societies of rudimentary organization. Except the Ifugaos, they are all in a very low state of civilization, dependent on a supply of their daily food from hand to mouth. The Eskimo may indeed be reckoned considerably above the lowest step if we consider the admirable adaptation of their instruments, the ingenuity of their appliances, and the skill and beauty of their ivory carvings. But the great test is their power of accumulating and laying up stores of food and other provisions, so that they may be able to rest on an artificial and well-thought-out basis of subsistence; and this test they fail to pass. Among all these peoples the seal of authority is found to rest in the people themselves, controlled by little definite organization. The beginnings of such an organization are, however, found in the family, an institution based upon the union of the sexes and the blood-kinship which thence ensues. In this form it is probably the earliest of human institu_ tions. But until it is provided with a distinct shape by the formation of clans, it seems incapable of further advance. In Australia alone of the cases we have examined has this advance been made. We shall now turn to a few typical examples of the constitution of society in the higher savagery and barbarism. The developments are numerous and varied ; and we shall not have space (nor is it necessary) to consider them at the same comparative length as the more elementary forms with which we have hitherto been dealing.

We will begin with the Yakuts, a people of the northeast of Siberia, one of the coldest regions of the habitable globe. Like most of those previously considered they are a nomadic people, but unlike them they have advanced to the accumulation of wealth in the shape formerly of droves of horses and now of cattle, from which their food and clothing are obtained. Their food-supply is therefore no longer the hand-to-mouth supply on the natural basis of hunting and fishing. Their organization rests on the *sib*, or kindred, now descendible in the male line, though formerly in the female line. The *sib* or clan is called *Aga-sesa*. It consists of an indefinite number of individuals all conceived as related by blood. The clans are grouped into a *nasleg*, and these again into an *ulus*, terms which may be translated respectively as *sub-tribe* and *tribe*. The clan is divided into families, dependent on the size of the droves belonging to them. The smallest drove, on which a family of four persons could barely subsist, was ten head, namely, five mares, one stallion, one two-year-old, one one-year-old, and two suckling foals. On the other hand, a maximum of from three hundred to five hundred head would maintain a community of

thirty in comparative ease. These economic conditions
on the Siberian steppes have severely limited not
merely the growth of population but the progress of
civilization. Whether large or small, the clan used to
be the community owning a drove ; and between the
members of the clan there was community of goods.
They dwelt in settlements or villages, each village being
surrounded by enough land for the pasturage of the
drove. The land of the tribe for this purpose is divided
among the sub-tribes, and the land of the sub-tribe
among the clans of the *nasleg*. It was re-allotted from
time to time with the view of meeting the fluctuating
requirements of the various divisions of the people,
for which special officials were appointed. There is a
strong feeling of solidarity within the *sib*, which formerly
blazed up in blood-feuds, and still shows itself on the
one hand in shielding wrong-doing by comrades, and on
the other hand by justice and right-doing within the
sib. Before the Russian occupation the whole clan was
held responsible for a murder by one member, and was
required to make compensation either in blood or
damages. Every *sib* has a council of elders that settles
all questions ; and whatever may be the character of
its decisions within the clan, as between its own members
and those of another clan it still takes the part of the
former. The powers of the head of the clan were
limited to the administration of justice and leadership
in war. A war or blood-feud, when it took place,
usually resulted, according to the national legends, from
the stealing of women or of the animal wealth of the
clan. Reconciliations were celebrated by meetings
with ceremonies and feasting. The clans were independent of one another. They used sometimes to make

alliances for defence or economic purposes. In summer, council meetings of the whole tribe are held in the open air, which are attended by every one ; but the decisions are arrived at by the elders, and accepted and confirmed by the assembly. By the Russian occupation and the introduction of cattle, which require much less labour and attendance than horses, the structure of Yakut society has been loosened and to a great extent revolutionized. The *kergen*, or family, takes the place of importance formerly held by the clan or *sib*. The solidarity of the *sib* has passed or is passing rapidly away. In the *kergen* the young are subjected to the elder, and all to the head, usually the father or (failing him) a brother, in whom all the property of the family is vested and who can dispose of it as he pleases. His power over the other members is uncontrolled. Thus the life of the Yakuts is passed in the care of their droves of horses or herds of cattle that find pasturage on the steppe ; and in the occasional pursuit of game or fishing. The organization and the conditions of life imply a generally peaceful environment, and hence a greater concentration of authority has been unnecessary and has not been developed.[1]

From the Yakuts we turn to the Melanesians, a people who also, in a very different climate and environment, have made considerable advances in civilization. Their wealth consists not in droves of horses or herds of cattle, but in their fields of yams and taro, their plantations of bread-fruit trees, and their pigs. They are even acquainted with the use of money, and have three species of currency—not, of course, of metal, but of

[1] " J. A. I.," XXXI, 65 *sqq.* ; Czaplicka, 55-62.

shells, of feathers, and of mats. The Melanesians are a mixed race, perhaps developed from negritoes and Papuans with larger or smaller infusions of immigrant (probably Malay) blood. They inhabit the islands eastward and south-eastward of New Guinea as far as, and including, the Fijian archipelago; and they have in comparatively recent times colonized the south-eastern shores of New Guinea itself. Taking the Banks' Islands as typical, the fundamental matter about Melanesian society is that it is divided into two kins, called *veve*, which are strictly exogamous. The division is not political; for members of both kins are found in every village, in every house. The *veve*, or kin, reckons descent through the mother only; and inside the kin there are families, some of which " have a certain family pride, and endeavour to keep up by intermarriage the family connexion." In this there is a germ, but only a germ of rank. There is no tribal organization. Each *veve* is subdivided into groups unconnected with the regulation of marriage. The islands are also divided into districts, often inhabited by people speaking obviously different dialects, having local autonomy. The relation of the groups into which the *veve* is divided with the districts has not been determined. Practically all the men are associated into connected societies or clubs, called respectively the *Sukive* and the *Tamate*. Entrance into these clubs is obtained by introduction through an existing member (usually the candidate's mother's brother) and the payment of sums of native money. Each is organized into various ranks, promotion in which is also obtained by payment. The higher ranks form a gerontocracy, only attainable by wealth and influence. This gerontocracy rules the people through the medium of the clubs. It is not, strictly speaking, hereditary. A father, however, would see to his son taking such degrees in the societies as would ensure his continuing his own dignity and authority. The beginnings of gerontocracy are observable among other savage people, especially among those who perform rites of initiation upon youths at puberty, and notably among the Australian natives. The Melanesians have elaborated these rites into more or less secret societies with a hierarchy of ranks applied to the purpose of government. Such an organization would not be possible without a settled community and an accumulation of wealth. Here also the general condition is one of peace, varied, however, by warlike expeditions, particularly on some of the islands by the amusement of head-hunting raids.[1]

The Polynesians (a race mainly of Malay origin, occupying the islands of the Pacific Ocean from Hawaii to New Zealand) are essentially warlike. Among the Maori the child, if a boy, was dedicated to the god of war ;[2] and his primary instruction was in the art of war.[3] The chiefs, it is said, used to spend the winter in plotting, with all the piety, callousness, and treachery of a Prussian king, the wars to be undertaken the following summer. In fact, the normal condition was one of war. This brought with it a more complex organization of society than any that we have considered hitherto. We find accordingly that the popu-

[1] Codrington, 21, 24, 25, 33, 54–58 ; Rivers, " Hist. Mel. Soc.," *passim.*
[2] Taylor, 186.
[3] Polack, II, 1.

lation was divided into three classes : the aristocracy
called *rangatira*, in which chiefs were included ; the
common people, *tàngata-ware* ; and the slaves, *pononga*
or *taurekareka*.   Bravery and eloquence, or persuasive
power, were the two qualifications most insisted on ;
and these were capable, by the influence they gave him,
of raising a man from the common people to the rank of
chief, which, on the other hand, his descendants would
lose if they were wanting in such qualities.[1]   According
to legend the ancestors of the Maori came to the
islands in three canoes.   The reputed descendants of
these ancestors were known by the names of the three
canoes respectively.   They constituted the   three
primary lateral divisions of the people.   They were
again divided into *iwi*, or tribes, according to their
subsequent legendary ancestors, and these into sub-
tribes, called *hapu*.[2]   The chief was the head of a tribe
or sub-tribe.   He had no influence beyond, unless in
war-time he were elected to lead a combination.   All
war-chiefs were chosen from recognized chiefs.   Apart
from election for this special purpose the dignity of
chief was strictly hereditary in the eldest child, or
failing him the next, and so on.   The heir was called
ariki, whether son or daughter, though a female *ariki*,
albeit she was very influential, could not lead in war
and lacked some of the privileges of the male *ariki*.
The Maori were devoted ancestor-worshippers ; hence
the *ariki* was not merely a chief with secular functions :
he was priest of his sacred ancestors as well.   This gave
him command of the most potent spells and the right
of precedence everywhere.   He was indeed, like the

[1] Shortland, 226 ; Taylor, 194, 355.
[2] *Ibid.*, 223 ; E. Tregear, " J. A. I." XIX, 97.

ancestors whose priest he was, sacred. Nay, every successive link in the genealogical chain was more sacred than those before it : every successive generation had two more illustrious ancestors than the preceding generation.[1] The chief, like every head of a household, was supreme over his own household. Outside it he had no power to compel ; and few matters of importance, domestic or foreign, could be undertaken except after public discussion and decision. At the assembly held for this purpose not only chiefs but also the warriors, women, and even children, were permitted to speak ; thus political wisdom and eloquence were early acquired. The final decision, however, rested with the chiefs. A chief might put to death any of his slaves ; but he stayed his hand before one of his wives or children, for the death of a wife might result in a claim by her kin for compensation, or in vengeance, and for the death of a child he would be liable to be called to account by his *hapu* or *iwi*.[2] His prestige depended partly on his personal qualities and conduct, and partly on those of his divine ancestors, with whom he was believed to be in constant communication. He was surrounded by a *tapu* which rendered his person inviolable, or even unapproachable, unless by a mightier and more illustrious personage.[3] The central force of Polynesian society was *tapu* (whence our English word *taboo*). Its power was so great that anything that belonged to, or even was touched by, a chief could only be touched afterwards by one less great than he at the risk of death by supernatural means.

---

[1] Tregear, *ibid.* 112 ; Shortland, 226.
[2] Polack I, 36, 54 ; II, 61 ; Shortland, 227.
[3] Polack, I, 27

3

His very name was sacred and not lightly to be pronounced. A chief could *tapu* any property to himself
by a word. The power he thus wielded over the
superstitions of the people was immense.[1] Public
quarrels between chiefs were referred to and decided
by the *rangátira nui*, or head of the tribe.[2] Of necessity
in a condition so unstable and so liable to surprise
attacks the population was gathered in *pas*, or stockaded
forts, the sites of which were chosen with great judgment,
and the defences of which were elaborated with care.
Indeed, military genius was developed that soon learned
to accommodate itself with not a little success to
the new firearms introduced by the *pakeha*, or white
man.[3]

Material reward of success in war does not seem
to have been sought, except in one direction : the
slaughtered foes were brought home to be the subjects
of a cannibal feast.   Thus was not only the last indignity
inflicted, but by eating the body of a conquered enemy
all his powers and all his qualities were appropriated by
the victor.   Beyond this, however, in a land where
there were few animals of any size fit for eating, and
where the natural basis of sustenance was still that of
the inhabitants, human flesh was a welcome if not
a necessary resource.[4] Maori cannibalism was not
entirely due to ferocity, but also, and perhaps yet more,
to the physical craving for diet more stimulating than
fish, fern-root, or taro. Beyond the Pacific Ocean a
similar craving seems to have led to cannibalism in

[1] Polack, I, 37; Shortland, 101; " J. A. I.," XIX, 113;
Taylor, 163 *sqq.*, 352.
[2] Polack, II, 63.
[3] Shortland, 245; Polack, II, 25.
[4] Taylor, 193, 352, 353; Shortland, 247, 251.

Mexico. The Aztecs are believed to have come from the far north-west. In so doing they must have traversed the Rocky Mountains and the great plains, both of them abounding in the big game of the North American Continent. Probably their sojourn there was no short one. So much the greater therefore was the change when they descended into what are now the southern provinces of the Mexican Republic, where the principal food was derived from the cultivation of maize, and their life was perforce changed from that of nomadic hunters to that of settled cultivators of the soil. They possessed no beasts of burden or draught, and no large domestic animals of any kind. For a stimulating diet they had recourse to human flesh. To provide it they waged continual warfare on the tribes they now found around them. In that warfare it was their great aim to take prisoners for sacrifice to their terrible gods, and after sacrifice to be eaten.[1]

Before dealing with the Aztecs, however, it is necessary to make clear the distinction between tribal organization and that of a State.

Tribal organization is founded upon the kin. No one can be recognized as a member of a tribal society who does not belong to one or other of the kindreds within it. A newborn child has no rights, and may be put to death or exposed and abandoned to the wild beasts and the mercies of external nature, until it has been received and accepted by the head of the kin. When this has been done it has more or less acquired the rights of a kinsman—rights which await confirmation when at or after the age of puberty the ceremonies are performed which are necessary to full recognition.

[1] Payne, II, 379, 380, 499–501.

Admission of an alien into the Iroquois tribe was by adoption by one or other of the kins in the tribe. It was frequently performed on prisoners taken in war and was the only alternative to torture and death. A regular ceremony was performed, in which usually a mother who has lost a son formally adopted a captive in his stead. He was by this rite admitted into the tribe, to which he henceforth belonged, and lost his status in the tribe of his birth.[1] A similar procedure was common in other North American tribes. The Osage rule, however, was that when a captive was to be received into the tribe the rite resembled a blood-covenant and several clans took part in it ; but the new member was adopted into the family of his captor.[2]

The blood-covenant is a very common ceremony in other parts of the world. It consists in the transfusion of blood between two or more individuals, either directly, or by drinking, or in some symbolic manner. By this means the persons who go through the rite and those whom they represent become of one blood, and are entitled to all the privileges and liable to all the duties of blood-kinship, exactly as if they had been born to them.

The transition from tribal organization to political organization takes place when one military tribe overcomes another and settles upon its territory. It is the incorporation of the conquered tribe in the new organization, the object of which is the maintenance of the military hold upon the land. The emphasis is transferred from the kindred to the country ; the conquered

---

[1] Morgan, " League," I, 331–334.
[2] F. La Flesche, " Holmes Anniv. Vol.," 287.

tribe ultimately coalesces with the conquerors and accepts the new outlook, the conquerors, on the other hand, taking the conquered as fellow-countrymen, and both finding in this new relation a common interest against all other peoples. The process usually occupies generations. When it is accomplished the " primitive " organization no longer exists : the tribe has been transformed into a kingdom, the tribesman has become a citizen, his admission is not by adoption or blood-covenant, but by an oath of allegiance and a formal recognition of his fellow-citizenship, he pays the dues and performs the obligations demanded by the sovereign power from the class of citizens he has entered, and is entitled to the same privileges and protection from the sovereign power as other members of the class.

When the Spaniards came they found the Aztecs in an advanced state of civilization. The soil was systematically cultivated, substantial houses of stone were built, gold was worked, the measurement of time for civil and religious purposes had reached the reckoning of 365 days to the year, chronological records were kept, picture-writing was developed, and arithmetical calculations were in use for various purposes, not the least important of which for the State was the assessing and recording of the tribute paid by the subject peoples. The Aztecs had descended upon Mexico, like the barbarians upon Rome, with a tribal organization. Their settlement there, their contact with more highly civilized nations as well as with the ruder aborigines, had changed the character of their organization. Surrounded on all sides by foes and peoples conquered but by no means assimilated, the leadership of the tribal chiefs was transformed into a great military despotism, though the transformation had not yet been fully completed.[1] The military aristocracy was organized under the monarch on feudal lines, the chiefs to whom lands were assigned on military tenure being compelled to reside at Mexico with their families, though always ready to take up arms. Out of the warrior class a military council for the sovereign was formed, and a judicial body. There was a court of first instance, with a right of appeal to higher judges, and thence to the sovereign himself. The whole power seems to have been in the hands of the warrior class, the heads of which formed the nobility. Below the warriors were the peasants, whose lives were a round of toil and taxation. Their burdens were all the greater for want of domestic animals. The cultivation of the land was perhaps the least. All the building materials were transported by the peasants, whose labour was also employed in building and repairing. They conveyed the produce of the lands they cultivated to the proper storehouses for the use of the warriors and religious officials, who had the first claim upon it ; they also transported the tributes of the subject peoples ; they attended the warriors on active service as bearers of their arms and food. Hardly less laborious than the peasants' was the life of the warrior class. Once in every period of two hundred days, as well as at other times when the sovereign willed, they were summoned to take the field and attack a hostile district, not because there was any just quarrel or any reason to forestall the enemy, but as a mere military exercise, and because the gods required human sacrifices and the cannibal warriors food. Both the

[1] Payne, II, 494.

warriors and the peasants were prescribed a rigorous course of education for the parts they had to sustain ; and their courses are pictured for us in the Mendoza Codex, prepared shortly after the conquest and now in the Bodleian Library at Oxford. The son was usually brought up in his father's occupation, from which he had no liberty to diverge. The gods, the sovereign, and the chiefs of the aristocracy were housed in splendid and substantial buildings. The people were gathered in *pueblos*, or villages, of which the most important was Mexico, where the sovereign resided. Everything was subordinated to the maintenance of military dominance, the keystone of which was the worship of their pitiless deities. It was a more than Prussian tyranny, though the unfortunate natives may well have doubted whether the God of the Holy Inquisition, who, by the Spanish conquest, supplanted Huitzilopochtli and Tezcatlipoca, was one whit less cruel or less addicted to feeding on human flesh than they ! [1]

In the west of Africa dwelt a people who had gone through a constitutional evolution very similar to that of the Aztecs, but who had not attained to quite so great a civilization, and whose continual wars resulted in prisoners and human sacrifices as bloody as theirs, though not in cannibalism—the people of Dahomey, West African negroes speaking an Ewhe speech, dialects of which are spoken all over the Slave Coast and its immediate interior. The constitution of an Ewhe tribe in general is that of an aristocracy of local chiefs, subject to the king as head of the tribe. The common people have no voice in the government. Dahomey was a military monarchy. The king had made himself

[1] *Ibid.*, II, 477 *sqq.*, 486 *sqq.*

absolute ; and all property belonged to him, even
the land which among other Ewhe belongs to the tribe.
He confiscated to himself whenever he pleased the
property of any individual. His person was sacred :
chiefs even of the highest rank were compelled to
prostrate themselves before him, face downward on
the earth, and throw dust over their heads. He had
a number of officials, of whom the principal were the
Megan or Muigan, his chief adviser and grand executioner, and the Mehu, his master of the ceremonies, who
collected his revenue. On the king's death temporary
anarchy ensued, during which all sorts of licence pre-
vailed and no one could be punished even for crimes.
It was ended as speedily as possible by the Megan and
Mehu, whose duty it was to select one of the king's sons
to succeed him. The eldest son had a prima facie
claim ; but he could be set aside and another appointed.
The king's harem was usually large and his children
were therefore numerous. To maintain discipline in
the palace there were a number of female officials
corresponding to the masculine officials of the court.
All officials, both those of the court and the provincial
authorities or chiefs, were appointed and removed by
the king at pleasure. When appointed, the king gave
an official the insignia of his office, which were required
to be returned when he died or ceased to hold office.
The local officials held courts for the trial of charges or
the decision of disputes, but the more important of these
were reserved for the higher authorities, or in the last
resort for the king. During the Annual Customs (the
hecatombs of human sacrifice that the king offered to
his divine ancestors), affairs of State and high politics
were discussed by him with his counsellors. At that

time the meanest slave had access to him for the purpose of making complaints, and it was frequently then that such matters were inquired into. Out of the king's revenue all his personal expenses and those of the State were defrayed. It was derived from taxation on local productions and all imports, collected in kind ; from the animal " gifts " made by the heads of families, traders, headmen of villages, and provincial chiefs at the Annual Customs ; from the sale of prisoners of war who were not put to death ; from the property of persons sentenced to death or slavery ; and lastly from the gifts of the provincial chiefs. These functionaries were not paid by the king ; but it was their business to extort as much as they safely could from the people under their jurisdiction, by means of real or imaginary charges, and therefrom to make their presents to the king. His power was maintained by means of a large standing army—the core of which was the three thousand Amazons, as the king's female bodyguard was called by Europeans—by the devotion of the officials throughout the kingdom (whose interest was the same as the king's), and by an extensive and elaborate spy-system.

This iron constitution, like the autocracies recently tyrannizing over the east and centre of Europe, exhibits the resources of a comparatively advanced civilization abused in the interests of the autocrat and a small band of officials to the enslavement of the rest of the people. In its external policy it was applied to raising and maintaining an immense military force, by means of which every year the neighbouring tribes were raided, terrorized, and conquered. It was the duty of the Amazons to go out on military service as well as to guard

the king and police the capital. Apart from them
there was no warrior class. When the king declared
war the male population was called out by messengers
sent through all parts of the kingdom. Each chief
at the head of the men of his own district took the
field, and along with them went the women to transport
ammunition and supplies, and if necessary to take part
in the fighting. They met at the capital and then set
forth, marching by night so as to surprise the foe
from whom the king proposed to take plunder and
prisoners, for these were the chief objects of his ordinary
expeditions. The plunder helped to fill the royal
treasury ; the prisoners provided the annual sacrifices
to his ancestors, the wholesale horror of which long
resounded in the reports of travellers and made the
name of Dahomey a byword of senseless cruelty throughout the world. It was no wonder that the French,
who held the protectorate of the adjoining coast
were compelled after long forbearance to intervene
in defence of territories they claimed and in vindication of common humanity, and to put an end once
for all to the kingdom and the rites of its bloodthirsty
gods.[1]

A parallel transformation from tribal organization
to that of the State was undergone during the Middle
Ages by the various peoples that in Europe invaded
and overcame the Roman Empire, or rose out of its
ashes. As a final illustration of " primitive " constitutional law we may take one of these. The Welsh
kingdoms were probably founded by a series of incursions
from the north, which were led by a more or less mythical
chief, Cunedda, and his sons. The conquest seems to

[1] Ellis, " Ewe," Chaps. XI and XII.

have been easy. The rival kingdoms which came into existence maintained for centuries desultory and fluctuating wars between themselves and against their encroaching Anglo-Saxon neighbours, until one of them succeeded in imposing some sort of an overlordship upon the rest. When Howel Dda, King of Deheubarth, reached this position early in the tenth century he apparently aimed at fusing the various realms, not merely by the rough-and-ready means of conquest or intermarriage of the royal houses, but by the more solid method of a common system of law. He was perhaps inspired by the example of Alfred the Great, who had previously codified the local Saxon laws. Be this as it may, the laws which have come down to us under the name of Howel Dda, though in their present form much later than the date of Howel himself, probably owed their origin to his reign ; and they afford us a picture of a society in process of change from tribal to civil conditions. " Looking at the system as a whole," says Sir John Rhŷs and Sir D. Brymnor Jones, " it must be described as still tribal. Political and property rights, as well as the status of individuals, depended upon a theory of blood-relationship. The whole community is looked upon as an aggregate of tribes or clans and families, forming a ruling aristocracy, under whom other classes of lower status are grouped. The form of government, so far as the term ' government ' can be used at all, was monarchical. In theory the king of Gwynedd or Aberffraw was head of the organization. He himself recognized the over-lordship of the King of England. Regularly, all other chieftains, princes or kings in Cymru were subject to the lord of Aberffraw. The result is that there was a more or less well-understood hierarchy of kings or princes, which presents remarkable analogies to a feudal kingdom."[1] The whole county was divided into *cantrefs*, and these into *cymwds*. The *cantref* was ruled by a lord appointed by the king. He had a set of officers corresponding to those of the royal household. Sometimes several *cantrefs* were combined under one lord, who called himself prince or king; but in any case, if we may judge from the laws, each *cymwd* and *cantref* maintained its separate organization. The lord delegated to certain officers the discharge of some of his functions. In every *cymwd* there was a *maer* and a *canghellor* discharging prescribed governmental duties, and in each *cymwd* a court was held by them with the aid of other officers."[2]

Thus far the organization as a State. But there was another and older organization, the tribal organization, which pervaded it and was not entirely superseded for ages. " The *cymry* of full blood deemed themselves descended from a common ancestor; but they were divided into numerous kindreds, each of which formed a kind of privileged oligarchy, but subordinate to the kindreds of royal status. The kindred [*cenedl*] was an organized and self-governing unit, having at its head a *penkenedl* [chief of the kindred]. The Welsh *cenedl* comprised the descendants of a common ancestor to the ninth degree of descent. The *penkenedl*, say the Laws, must not be either a *maer* or *cangellor* of the king, but an *uchelwr* [nobleman] of the country; and his status must not be acquired by maternity. He has to pay a tribute yearly to the *arglwydd* [lord] or higher chieftain.

---

[1] Rhŷs and Jones, " Welsh People," 188.
[2] *Ibid.*, 190.

He must be an efficient man, being the eldest of the
efficient men of the kindred and being the chief of a
household, or a man with a wife and children by legitimate marriage. He was assisted by three other officers :
the representative, whose duty was to mediate in Court
and assembly, and in combat within the tribe, and to
act for the kindred in every foreign affair ; the avenger,
who led the kindred to battle, and pursued evil-doers,
brought them before the Court, and punished them
according to its sentence ; the avoucher, who seemingly
entered into bonds and made warranty on behalf of the
kindred."[1] The kindred was thus " an aggregate of
families residing in separate homesteads, at the head of
each of which was a *pentenlu* [chief of the household],"
who was assisted for various purposes by the officers
and a council of elders. All these families were held to
be descended from a common ancestor. There were,
however, different classes of persons, or castes ; and
status depended on birth.[2] The primary distinction
was between tribesmen or non-tribesmen, men of Cymric
or non-Cymric blood. Those of Cymric blood were
divided into a royal class, belonging to kindreds of kingly
or princely status ; the nobility ; and innate tribesmen
called *boneddigion*, gentlemen. Below these were the
unfree, that is to say, the villeins and the slaves.[3]
The nobility and *boneddigion* were liable to military
service at any time within the country, and for six
weeks in the year outside it. As in the Mexican constitution, there were provisions for the education of
youth. From the age of fourteen, until when the boy
was maintained by his father, he was commended to
the lord (originally, it is suggested, to the head of the

[1] *Ibid.*, 192.   [2] *Ibid.*, 193.   [3] *Ibid.*, 191.

kindred) into whose protection he was received, whose man he became, and to whom he became liable for military service. The lord fulfilled his duty by handing him over to a *taeog*, one of the unfree classes, on whom he thus became quartered during this period, and with whom he lived in fosterage. Ultimately he became a fully qualified adult and received his share of the ancestral land.[1]

Below the *boneddigion* the unfree classes were incapable of bearing arms and of horsemanship, and their evidence was of no value against the classes above them. The *taeog*, or villein, could not possess family land, but had rights of occupation of servile land.[2] It may be conjectured, however, that the position gradually, if slowly, improved in course of time. There was also a great distinction between laymen and clerics. The latter, while enjoying certain immunities or privileges, were also subject to some disqualifications. The Church possessed a good deal of land granted from the tribal stock, or by the lord.[3] Churchmen had their own courts, and were exempt from the jurisdiction of the civil courts, though they might sue laymen in them. These privileges generally agreed with those that the Church struggled everywhere so persistently throughout the Middle Ages to attain.[4]

The highest lay court was that of the king or prince, to which, in addition to jurisdiction in certain disputes touching the king, or his household, there was an appeal from the local courts of the *cantref* and the *cymwd*. The laws among other things lay down minutely the number, duties, order of precedence, maintenance, and perquisites of the officers of the royal household, the

[1] *Ibid.*, 205 *sqq.*   [2] *Ibid.*, 214.   [3] *Ibid.*, 216.   [4] *Ibid.*, 217.

value of the testimony of various classes of the community, the penalties for insult, injury, and killing of the members of different classes, the rights of the king to entertainment and contribution for himself and his retinue on progress, the rights of the kin to vengeance for the death of a member and their liability to contribute to the fine of any member for a crime—all of them notes of the transition of society from a tribal condition to that of a modern civilized state [1]

[1] Wade-Evans, " Welsh Medieval Law," *passim*.

CHAPTER III

PERSONAL RIGHTS AND LIABILITIES

WE have next to consider the rights as between themselves of the component members of a relatively primitive society. Here the first observation to be made is that, at all events in the societies that have been most fully investigated, the unit is not the individual but the kin. The individual is but part of the kin. If he be injured, it is the kin which is injured. If he be slain, it is the blood of the kin that has been shed, and the kin is entitled to compensation or to vengeance. If he commit a wrong, the whole kin is involved ; and every member is liable, not as an individual, but as part of the kin that committed the wrong.

In Australia, Africa, and America the kin usually takes shape as a totemic clan. A totemic clan is a body of real or reputed kinsmen named from some animal, plant, or occasionally from some other phenomenon, with which its members claim a mystical connexion. Often the clan is believed to be descended from the object whose name it bears. If that object be an animal or plant the entire species is sacred. Every member of the animal species is held to be related to the clan, and no member of the clan will

48

ordinarily take its life or eat of it ; and frequently, on the other hand, it is regarded as exercising some sort of protective influence over its human clients or relatives.

This object is called the *totem*, a word derived from the Algonkian languages of North America, and expressive of brother-sister kinship. The descent of a totemic clan is counted through one side only, either the father or the mother; originally, there is reason to believe, everywhere through the mother. Intermarriage between members of the clan is strictly forbidden : this is the rule of exogamy. Sometimes clans band together in phratries which are held to have a near relationship with one another. When this is the case there are usually two phratries in a tribe, and intermarriage is then permitted only between members of opposite phratries. The rule in question holds good in general for the North American totemic tribes. The Australian exogamic institutions, described in a previous chapter, seem to be a development from it.

In South Africa the totemic organization had long been decadent. It is probable that exogamy has ceased to be observed by the Bechuana, though it maintains an existence among the Zulus and some other tribes.[1] Farther north the organization is in greater strength, though in many tribes, in consequence of the tendency to reckon descent through the father instead of the mother (which is believed to have been the original reckoning of all totemic peoples), it is undergoing a transformation. A consequence of this among the Baganda and their neighbouring peoples is that a man is prohibited from marrying into either his father's

[1] Frazer, " Totemism and Exogamy," II, 378, 382.

or his mother's clan.[1]   The peoples of Central Africa who are not Bantu are not all divided into totemic clans.   Where they are organized on a clan basis they in general observe the rule of exogamy.[2]   The same may also be said of the negroes of West Africa.[3]

The aboriginal tribes of India are also organized in totemic clans, or where not now so organized they display remains of a former clan-system.   Exogamy is a usual feature of the system.   Totemic clans are also the basis of society in some parts of Indonesia and in Melanesia.   Exogamy is generally found with the totemic organization ; but in many of the Melanesian islands society is organized in marriage-classes on lines analogous to, but less complex than, those of Australia, and the exogamic rule attaches to these classes rather than to the totemic clans.[4]

In the absence or breakdown of the clan-organization exogamy takes a different form : it is often regulated by locality.   A man may not then marry a woman of his own district, or his own village.   Thus, in the Kulin tribe in what is now the colony of Victoria, Australia, the wife had to be found from a distance ; and, among their neighbours and kinsmen the Kurnai, a man might not marry a woman of his own district : his choice was limited to women of certain districts who had by tradition *connubium* with that to which he belonged. Here it is probable the exogamic regulations were not unconnected with the clan-organization.   Descent was traced through the father ; and the Australian rule,

[1] Frazer, "Totemism and Exogamy," II, 453, 456, 458, 462, 473.
[2] *Ibid.*, 448, 419, 427.
[3] *Ibid.*, 562, 579.
[4] *Ibid.*, Chaps. V, VI, VII, IX, and X, *passim*.

which required the wife to go to her husband's camp
and reside there with him, had the effect of congre-
gating together the clansmen, so that one clan would
occupy one district and a different clan another district.
Hence the districts having *connubium* would probably
be districts settled by different clans and thus inter-
marriageable.[1] More strictly local was the exogamy
of the Panches of Bogotu, of whom it is related that the
men and women of one town did not intermarry, but
if a sister were born in a different town from her brother
he was not prevented from marrying her.[2] The Orang
Laut of the Malay Peninsula, who formerly lived by the
sea, are said to have taken wives only from another
community than their own.[3] It may, however, be
suspected that in all cases of local exogamy the original
reason was to avoid marrying into the same kin. It is
expressly said of the Panches that the men and women
of one town held themselves to be brothers and sisters,
and " the impediment of kinship was sacred to them."
The tribes of the Upper Amazons, who live in small
communities in the primeval forests, each community
in a common dwelling, have a preference for marrying
within the tribe ; yet exogamy is very strictly enforced
as regards the community, because " all within the
household are held to be kin."[4] So of the Mafulu of
New Guinea we are told : " Marriages are usually
contracted with women of another community, though
sometimes the wife will belong to another clan in the

[1] Howitt, 146, 252, 269, 272, 273. Cf. Hartland, " Primitive Society," 79, 81.

[2] Tylor, " J. A. I." XVIII, 268, citing Piedrahita, " Historia
Generál de las Conquistas del Nuévo Reynode Granáda."

[3] Skeat and Blagden, II, 86.

[4] Whiffen, 66–67.

same community. Very rarely only is she of another
village of the same clan, and still more rarely is she of
the same village, clan-exogamy being the rule, and
marriages within the clan, and still more within the
village, being regarded as irregular and undesirable,
and people who have contracted them being considered
as having done wrong."[1]

As an alternative to local exogamy there is found in
other tribes which have no clan-organization a prohibition to marry any person who has an ancestor in
common with the other spouse as far back as can be
ascertained, or (as some tribes forbid) for a certain
number of generations. What may have been the
cause of these prohibitions is still undetermined. Every
hypothesis hitherto offered by anthropologists is
unsatisfactory, and the problem need not detain us.
Certain it is, however, that the sense of kindred begins
to widen, even on a low plane of culture, beyond the
kinship acknowledged in the clan-system. The ties
of nature are recognized in the relations of daily life
before the mechanism of birth, through which these ties
originate, is understood, and probably before they
are imperfectly formulated in the clan-system. The
prohibition to marry near kin follows their recognition.

When society is organized by clans the members of a
clan are considered between themselves as brothers and
sisters. Their duty to one another is one of mutual
defence and support. An offence against one is an
offence against all, and immediately unites the clan
against the offender and his clan. For, conversely, the
offence of one member is the offence of all. If a

[1] Williamson, " Mafulu," 168.

member of the clan be killed, by so much is the strength of the clan reduced. Compensation must therefore be obtained either by corresponding reduction of the strength of the offending clan by the death of a member, or as civilization advances by a payment of goods or money. This kind of compensation is comparatively late. In low stages of civilization revenge by the slaughter of one of the offending clan is the rule. Nor does it matter that the revenge is on the person of one whom we should regard as entirely innocent : it is enough that he belongs to the offending clan. It is the duty of every member of the clan offended to exact revenge ; and the responsibility of the injury rests not merely on the actual individual offender but, by virtue of the solidarity of the clan as the social unit, on every member of his clan.[1]

Thus begins a blood-feud, which may last for generations. Indeed, it begins not necessarily from a deed of violence, but sometimes from a purely imaginary wrong. " Amongst the Central Australian natives there is no such thing as belief in natural death ; however old or decrepit a man or woman may be when this takes place, it is at once supposed that it has been brought about by the magic influence of some enemy, and in the normal condition of the tribe the death of an individual is followed by the murder of someone else who is supposed to be guilty of having caused the death."[2] As the account of the proceedings of an avenging party shows, the vengeance is wreaked in such a case not of necessity on the person who is supposed to be guilty but upon one of his clan, or even, where the

[1] Fison and Howitt, " Kamilaroi and Kurnai," 157.
[2] Spencer and Gillen, " Central Tribes," 476.

guilt is laid at the door of another tribe it is enough
to avenge it upon one of that tribe. At first every
member of the offending clan is subject to such vengeance, but as civilization advances the right of
vengeance is gradually limited. ◀Women and children
are often, for instance, exempted. As clans decay,
only the offender and his immediate kin remain liable,
and only the immediate kin according to their nearness
of blood are responsible for pursuing vengeance and
entitled to the fruits.

The clan-system, however, makes no provision for
a wrong inflicted by one member of the same clan
upon another. The clan cannot pursue a member of
its own body with vengeance. Yet serious misdeeds
may be committed by members of the clan on one
another, such as, in addition to homicide, adultery, rape,
theft, and other crimes which are apt to lead to
quarrels.

Where it is possible, the acts complained of are doubtless ignored, or they may be recognized as part of the
customs of the tribe. So in Samoa it " was not wrong
to steal from the plantation of a relative ; in fact, it
was not called stealing." We are told : " The indus-
trious man may work, whilst the lazy relative may help
himself to the fruit of his labours." As between
relatives, in fact, there was what was in effect a kind of
communism. The organization of society in Samoa has
passed, or is passing, out of the clan-system in which
such a custom probably began, and the right of the
clansman to the fruits of another clansman's labour,
or another clansman's property, has concentrated in
the family.[1] Some such explanation may perhaps

[1] Brown, " Melanesians and Polynesians," 262, 263, 264.

account for the similar liberties which are allowed to uterine nephews in more than one of the Bantu tribes of Africa.[1]

Where, however, a wrong cannot be ignored, as in the case of a turbulent and defiant member of the clan, it may still be possible for a general assembly of the clan to cast him off and outlaw him, a proceeding that we shall consider under the head of " Sanctions." The Kiwai of New Guinea have discovered another mode of dealing with the doer of a wrong, which, by reason of his being a clansman, tribal law does not permit them to avenge, or when he is, though not a clansman, so powerful a member of the community that they dare not. The difficulty is solved by employing another person, who is not forbidden by tribal law or not afraid of incurring the hostility of the wrong-doer, to carry out the punishment. To do this the person wronged or the person on whom the duty lies of avenging the wrong sends a gift of weapons to the substitute he has chosen. In a small community the wrong that has been done is usually notorious. Hence the person to whom the weapons are sent understands the gift without a word being said and its acceptance is an undertaking to perform what is required. He keeps the weapons until he has fulfilled the undertaking and then, after being paid for his services, he returns them.[2] But we are not told whether the consequence is to start a new blood-feud.

After the slaughter of a number of kinsmen on both sides in a blood-feud the participants gradually get tired of the state of hostility, and of themselves, or by

[1] See *infra*, p. 64.
[2] A. P. Lyons, " Man," XXI, 24–27.

the assistance of friends on both sides, make a ceremonial pact of peace, in which the number of victims
is reckoned up ; and sometimes one or more marriages
between the contending kins may seal the bargain, or
payment may be made by way of compensation.
Finally, as we shall see hereafter, payment for bloodshed
becomes the customary sanction. The liability for the
payment falls on the clan of the original wrong-doer,
unless the toll of lives taken in the feud is heavily
against them. When the clan-system has decayed
the liability rests on the family of the culprit, each
of whom has to contribute in proportion to his nearness
in blood. When it is made, the payment is shared
among the clansmen or, as the case may be, among the
more immediate kin of the slaughtered or injured man
in similar proportions. An example of these payments
for homicide may be taken from the mediaeval Welsh
laws. They are of great complexity. First it should
be noted that ecclesiastics who are related to either
party neither pay nor receive any portion of the murder-
fine ; nor does any person who is a monk, or leprous,
or dumb, or an idiot : and all such persons are prohibited from taking vengeance for any relative murdered,
nor are they liable to vengeance as of the kin of the
murderer. The murder-fine, called the *galanas*, is
divided into three parts, one of which is known as the
murderer's third. This is paid by the culprit himself,
his father, his mother, and his brothers and sisters, the
murderer being actually liable for no more than one-
third of it ; the other two-thirds of the murderer's
third are paid by his father, mother, brothers, and
sisters in equal shares, save that a woman only pays
one-half of a man's share. The whole of the murderer's

one-third share of the *galanas* is paid to the victim's parents and his brothers and sisters. The remaining two-thirds of the *galanas* are imposed on the culprit's remoter kin, and are paid as to two-thirds by his father's kin and as to one-third by his mother's kin, beginning with a first cousin, who is reckoned as the fifth remove from the murderer, down to the fifth cousin, who is reckoned as the ninth remove from the murderer ; and it is received by the corresponding kinsmen on the side of the victim. The rule of such payments is that every successive generation nearer to the murderer or murdered pays or receives double the amount of the generation next below it. The wife gets no part of the *galanas*, nor does she pay any. The children of the murderer or murdered are equally exempt. In the one case the murderer's payment stands for them as well as himself ; in the other case the care of them falls on their immediate kin who receive the payment. But the Welsh law recognized over and above the *galanas* what was called the *sarhâd*, a payment by the murderer and his kindred for the insult involved in the murder. Of this the victim's widow, if any, gets one-third ; the other two-thirds are received by his father and mother, brothers and sisters.[1]

These elaborate rules are in a very late stage. While they are manifestly derived from older laws relating to the clan and its claim for vengeance or compensation, the clan itself has disappeared ; the claim for compensation depends upon the more immediate kindred in the precise measure in which the members are related to the victim, according, in general terms, to modern

---

[1] Wade-Evans, " Welsh Medieval Law," 185, 346. Cf. Rhŷs and Jones, " The Welsh People," 228 *sqq*.

reckoning of propinquity. And the liability to compensation is measured in the same way and is attached to corresponding relatives of the murderer. The claim to vengeance and the liability to it attach to the same circle of kinsmen, and are in all respects precisely complementary.

I have spoken of murder throughout. But it must be remembered that no distinction is made by "primitives" between murder with malice aforethought and accidental, or even justifiable, homicide. Every case of bloodshed demands vengeance, for the honour as well as the integrity of the clan is involved. Considerable progress in civilization is made before the distinction in question is drawn. The Greeks do not seem to have drawn it when the Homeric poems were written. The Hebrews, however, in the late form in which their legislation has come down to us, recognized the distinction ; and in all their codes careful provision is made for determining the guilt or innocence, from the point of view of the intention of the manslayer. Cities of refuge are appointed to which he may flee, and where he shall be temporarily safe from the pursuit of the avenger of blood. Before the avenger of blood can touch him he is to be solemnly tried by " the congregation." If declared innocent, he is to be restored to the city of refuge to which he has fled, there to reside until the death of the high priest, when he will be permitted to return to " the land of his possession." But if at any time earlier he go beyond the bounds of the city of refuge and the avenger of blood find him, he may slay him without guilt. On the other hand, if the manslayer upon trial be declared guilty of wilful murder, he is to be delivered "into the hand of the avenger of blood, that he may die " [1] This is a great step forward, though the exile of the manslayer for a period, possibly of years, until the death of the existing high priest, and a strict limitation of his movements to the city of refuge, are a concession to the ancient demand for revenge for any death, however unpremeditated.

The advance is not unconnected with the decay, leading to the ultimate disappearance, of the clan. The clan on decay is not immediately succeeded by the individual as the unit of society. The cause of its decay is (apart from political events, such as those arising from the clash of two or more peoples having different institutions, or other circumstances) the growing consciousness of closer blood-ties than those of the clan.

This consciousness expresses itself in the terms of relationship which arise while the clan is yet in full strength and persist beyond its dissolution. The clan gives way to the family, a smaller and generally more closely knit body of kinsmen, which takes over its solidarity and joint responsibility. Gradually concentrating the responsibility on the actual manslayer or other culprit on the one side, and on the " avenger of blood " or other pursuer acting on behalf of the immediate relatives of the slaughtered man (" his father's house "), or in case of any other crime on behalf of the individual wronged *and* his family, on the other side, it finally dissolves the solidarity and leaves the individual as the now recognized unit of society for all purposes. This, however, is the result of a long evolution, accelerated or retarded by a variety of causes,

---

[1] Exod. xxi, Num. xxxv, Deut. xix.

and can hardly be predicated of any " primitive " community.

The family relationships fall next to be considered. The foundation of the family is the conjugal union of man and woman. Humanity having slowly emerged from a pre-human condition, naturally no records remain to testify to the early development of sexual relations. Those relations had become more or less permanent among all peoples at the stage at which we first meet with them in scientific inquiry or in the accounts of travellers and missionaries. Their very legends assume their existence as a standing institution, and only here and there refer to a more fleeting connexion as the rule among their long-departed progenitors, or among some strange and probably hostile aliens. Notwithstanding this, the forms of the conjugal connexion are so various that they seem to point to the emergence of marriage out of a condition little removed from promiscuity. We need not, however, enter into the speculations and controversies on this subject. Sexual relations are regulated, as well as other relations, even in the lowest human societies. We may illustrate the form of regulation by a few examples.

In general the savage lays no embargo upon the gratification of the sexual impulse by the unmarried youth of either sex, provided the rule of exogamy or that of prohibited degrees be not violated, and subject in some cases to prior initiation into adult life by the puberty ceremonies. Chastity has no value *per se* ; and virginity in a bride is rarely insisted on, save where a marriage-price has to be paid and is enhanced by it. The case is altered by marriage. Jealousy develops, usually but not always more strongly on the part of the husband. Among the Bantu the penalty for adultery is the death of the wife's seducer, and often of the erring wife. This severity is rendered necessary by the polygyny in which these races indulge. Among the Bantu of West Africa the severity is emphasized by the wide definition given to adultery. Miss Kingsley says it is " often only a matter of laying your hand, even in self-defence from a virago, on a woman, or brushing against her on the path. These accusations of adultery are, next to witchcraft, the great social danger to the West Coast native, and they are often made merely from motives of extortion or spite, and without an atom of truth in them." [1] Miss Werner, speaking particularly of the Yao and Angausa, says : " The man may be (and frequently is) shot or speared by the husband ; the wife is frequently let off with a warning the first time, but for a second offence either killed or divorced and sent back to her relatives, who in such a case must return whatever present was made at the marriage. . . . But in practice the matter is often arranged by paying damages, or the guilty man may be sold into slavery." [2] In both these cases descent is traced through the mother only. A fortiori, where the tracing of descent through the father only has arisen, masculine jealousy might be supposed to be emphasized. This, however, does not appear to be so. The civilized fear of tainting the offspring does not enter into savage consideration. The marriage ceremonies of many modern savages include the requirement that the bride shall submit to the

[1] Kingsley, " Travels," 497. Cf. Bastian, " Loango Küste," I, 168.
[2] Werner, " Brit. Cent. Afr.," 265.

embraces of a number of men before she reaches the
arms of her bridegroom.   The Arunta bride undergoes
repeated sexual intercourse with several men, beginning
with some belonging to marriage-classes with whom
intercourse is forbidden at all other times.[1] In antiquity the Nasamones and the Augilæ, both Cyrenaic
tribes, as well as the Balearic islanders, compelled the
bride to submit to intercourse with all the male wedding
guests.[2]   Moreover, the husband has often the right
and the custom to lend his wife to other men by way of
hospitality and for other reasons.   In particular, it
is not infrequent that he does so for the express purpose
that they may beget children for him.   The sacred law
of Manu lays down the rules to be observed and
the persons to whom the wife can be lent for this
purpose.[3]

The practice was well known to the ancient Arabs,
and is extensively used in Africa.[4]   The offspring of such
embraces are reckoned to the husband, though not a
drop of his blood flows in their veins.   There are also
ceremonial occasions on which general licence is a part
of the religious rites, as on several of the Molucca
Islands and elsewhere.

The truth is that descent through the father is a legal
fiction.   The definition of adultery in the lower culture
differs from ours.   So long as the marriage subsists

[1] Spencer and Gillen, " Central Tribes," 92 *sqq.*, 107 ; *ibid.*
" Northern Tribes," 133 *sqq.*

[2] Pomponius Mela, I, 8 ; " Diod. Sic.," V, 1.

[3] " Sacred Books of the East," XXV, 327–338 ; cf. II, 267,
302, 303.

[4] Robertson Smith, " Kinship," 110 *sqq.* ; " J. A. I.," XI,
171 *sqq.*, XLV, 295 ; N. W. Thomas, *ibid.* IV, 58, 60, 83, 130 ;
Mrs. Talbot, " Woman's Mysteries," 93, 211 ; Rehse, 93 ;
Junod, " South Africa Tribe," I, 210, 343.

the husband considers that he has, subject to the requirements of native law, the exclusive right to the use of
his wife, or to the disposal of her body. What he
complains of is her disposal of it without his consent or
the compulsion of social or religious tradition. Over
and over again the infringement of this right is called
in so many words "stealing," and treated as such.
The wife's paramour, unsanctioned either by the husband
or by native law, is the thief who has invaded and
appropriated the property of the husband. Both he
and the wife are often liable to death, though the wife
is usually let off with a less punishment, or even for-
given, while the full weight of the consequences—death
or a more or less substantial fine—falls on her partner in
guilt. Repeated infidelity, however ends in punishment
or dissolution of the marriage. But the moral question
—the question of chastity—is not raised : it is foreign
to the ideas of these stages of civilization. Nor is it
unusual among many peoples to exchange wives, not
merely upon occasion but for weeks at a time (as among
the Eskimo), or even permanently. It is difficult to
generalize amid the wide differences of custom.

In some instances objection seems not to be raised
to a special class of lover. Among the Santals, a
Dravidian tribe in India, a man's younger brother may
share his wife with impunity, provided their relations
are not public. It has been conjectured that this is a
relic of fraternal polyandry.[1] To the Masai of East
Africa adultery is an idea unknown. Masai society is
organized in "ages," or periods of about seven and a
half years ; and it is no offence for a man to have

[1] Risley, "Tribes and Castes of Bengal," Ethnog. Glossary,
II, 229.

intercourse with a woman—even a married woman—
belonging to his own " age." [1]   More to the south the
Thonga tribe, though reckoning kinship through the
father only, possesses many relics of a former uterine
descent.   Among these relics are the close relations
between a maternal uncle and his nephew.   The nephew
in certain contingencies inherits his uncle's widows—
a right he is accustomed to anticipate whenever he
chooses.   Even before his uncle's death he calls these
ladies " wives " and they call him " husband."   He is
entitled to amuse himself with any of them as a betrothed lover—a privilege which extends very far.
When he visits his uncle he deposits his sleeping-mat
in the hut of the wife of his preference, and stays with
her so long as he sojourns at the kraal. [2]   If we may
judge from their tales, the Haida of Queen Charlotte's
Islands, on the north-western coast of America, were
even more complaisant.   We find there uncles expressly
putting their wives at their nephews' disposal. [3]   It is
probable that in such cases as these we have examples
of the solidarity of the clan.   The entire clan, or family
as the case may be, has probably contributed to the
bride-price paid for these wives, and its members have
consequently claims upon them which the husband
is bound to recognize.   This would not apply to the
Masai.   But there a very close bond unites the brethren
of the same " age," and on the marriage of one of them
his companions often claim priority of intercourse
with the bride. [4]

[1] Hollis, " Masai," 261, 312.

[2] Junod, " Baronga," 77.   Cf., however, *ibid.*," South Africa
Tribe," I, 227, 228.

[3] " Jesup Exped.," X, 604, 746.

[4] Merker, 49.

We have no space to consider the conjugal relations of the lower culture in detail. It may, however, be said that, while jealousy on the part of either spouse is probably less developed than in the more civilized races, and while morals in this as well as other directions are certainly less developed, marriage, the more or less permanent union of man and woman, is everywhere found, and the derogations from the exclusive relations of husband and wife are also the subject of customs which have the force of law and are fully understood in the community bound by them. The various forms of marriage are polyandry, usually fraternal as in Tibet and the south of India, by which a woman is married to a band of brothers; polygyny, by which a man takes simultaneously or one after another as he pleases a number of women as wives, a practice much favoured in Africa, but common in the case of chiefs and wealthy men everywhere; and monogamy, the union of one man with one woman, which is, in practice, the lot of most men and women the world over.

The manner of entering into marriage varies greatly. It is frequently arranged by a previous betrothal. In this case the consent of parents or relatives is required. It is not uncommon among many peoples to betroth mere children, even to betroth them before birth conditionally upon the sex being suitable. It is said that an adult Carib will sometimes bespeak an unborn babe, and in such cases he paints the mother's body with a red cross. If the child prove a girl, this is a sufficient betrothal. Among the same people cousins of the opposite sexes, if on the mother's side, are reported to have been considered as betrothed as soon as they were born. Where maternal descent prevails, and in some cases under paternal descent, the parties have greater choice. Marriage is then preceded by wooing, of which sexual intercourse is generally a part. The final marriage is in most cases public and with the definite concurrence of the kin on both sides. The payment of a bride-price is common. It is not a purchase of the bride, but of the right to cohabitation, with the consequence often of the transfer from the wife's kin to the husband of the offspring of the marriage. The payment is not necessarily completed before the ceremony—sometimes not for years afterwards : it is enough if it be stipulated and an earnest paid. An extreme example of delay in full payment is the custom in two contiguous districts of the island of Sumatra, in which, when the two families concerned continue on good terms, the balance of the *jujur*, or bride-price, remains sometimes unadjusted to the second and third generation, and it is not uncommon to see a man suing for the *jujur* of the sister of his grandfather." [1]　Another important and beneficent effect of the payment of a bride-price, as among the Bantu of South Africa, is that it constitutes the kin of the bride, who receive shares, her protectors ever on the watch to prevent ill-usage by the husband in whose kraal she lives, and it operates as a caution to the husband, who dare not drive her into separation and refusal to return to him, because he knows that in such a case her kin would be united in her support, and he would lose both his wife and the bride-price he had paid for her.[2]

[1] Marsden, 259.

[2] About forty years ago the Cape Government held an exhaustive inquiry into this and other native laws and customs and reported fully upon them. See the report and evidence, Cape Town, 1883, *passim*.

Marriage by capture of the bride is a form found in many places. There are, or were not very long ago, relics of it to be found even in Europe. How far such a form is to be traced to hostile capture, like that of the Sabine women, has been much debated. While hostile capture has been undoubtedly practised in the past, and perhaps still is to some extent, most cases that have come under scientific investigation are those of brides taken by one kin from another in regard to which there is no hostile feeling and consequently no hostile capture. As a form of marriage they are usually preceded by consent on both sides, and often they are more of the nature of elopements than of capture. The reluctance on the part of the bride or her clan is more or less simulated. Where there is real reluctance, it is to be put down to that of a girl going to a life among unknown, or little known, people and the terror of a mother-in-law, or else to the feeling of being parted from her female relatives and friends, and on their side of losing a companion of their own sex.

A very archaic method of obtaining a wife is by exchange for a sister. By this means two men would be fitted with wives. The exchange of sisters is a practice largely followed in Australia, where the stage of civilization is too low to have developed the bride-price. It is found also in Baluchistan and among the non-Aryan tribes of India, also in New Guinea and the Western Islands of Torres Straits, in the French Soudan, and among the peasantry of Palestine. It must be regarded as a species of barter where payment for a bride is either unknown or beyond the means of a bridegroom. Seeing, moreover, that kinship in most of these cases is reckoned on what is called the classi-

ficatory system, a larger number than the offspring of
the same parents is included as sisters, and consequently there would be greater choice of persons. Sir
James Frazer has recently shown some reason for
believing that such a practice may have originated
the very common practice of the marriage of cross-
cousins—that is, the marriage of a brother's child to a
sister's child. Under the classificatory system the
children of brothers or the children of sisters, according
as descent is reckoned through the father or through
the mother, are brothers and sisters. As such they
would come under the law of exogamy and would be
ineligible for marriage among themselves. But cross-
cousins who are related to a common grandparent
through parents of opposite sexes stand, as Sir James
Frazer puts it, on a wholly different footing. Whether
kindred be reckoned through the father only or the
mother only, such cousins would belong to different
clans and so be marriageable ; and this qualification
has in many cases been continued by the system of
prohibited degrees which has supplemented exogamy
or taken its place. Where the marriage of cross-
cousins is permitted it is usually regarded as the best
kind of marriage. It gathers up and promotes family
feeling ; and among peoples that have made advances
in civilization it has the additional recommendation
of helping to preserve family property in, or at all
events in the second generation to return it to, the
family.[1]

Marriage does not necessarily involve the taking of
the bride away from her home to live with her husband.
Among many tribes they do not even live together :

[1] Frazer, " F. L. Old Test.," II, 205 *sqq.*

the husband simply visits his wife. This is the arrangement among the Nāyars of India,[1] the Syntengs of Assam,[2] the Orang Mamaq of Sumatra,[3] and previous to the fourteenth century the Japanese.[4] In all such cases the woman is the important member of the household ; she or her mother rules it, and descent is reckoned through her and not through the man. Visiting gradually expands into the permanent residence of the husband with the wife and her family. Even then he does not always become the head of the household : he is subject to his wife and her family, and often finds the servitude insupportable. When this is so, some peoples provide a way out of the difficulty by accepting a bride-price, or an increased bride-price if a bride-price has been already paid or agreed on, as a consideration for allowing the husband to carry off his wife and children. This generally, but not always, involves a change in the reckoning of descent : it is then reckoned through the father and not through the mother. In fact, we find almost all possible stages of the transition between the stage, certainly very early and apparently the earliest to which we are able to penetrate, in which the husband merely visits the wife and has no authority in the household or over the children, and that in which he is absolute master of the household and of his wives and children, and descent is reckoned through him.

Though supposed to be a permanent status, marriage

[1] Anantha Krishna, II, 22 *sqq.* ; Thurston, " Tribes and Castes," V, 152 *sqq.*, 283 *sqq.*
[2] Gurdon, " Khasis," 76.
[3] Wilkin, " Verspreide Geschriften," I, 314 ; " Bÿdragen," XXXIX, 43, 44.
[4] " L'Année Soc.," VIII, 422.

is hardly ever indissoluble. An end is capable of being put to it by separation almost everywhere. The will of the parties, or of one of them only, is often sufficient. In Arabia, even long since the promulgation of Islam, the women of some tribes might marry as they pleased, but the tent and all that was in it belonged to the wife. The husband might depart when he liked. In such a case he left the tent and its furniture with his wife, who undertook the whole charge of any children there might be of the marriage. Or, conversely, the wife had a right to dismiss her husband—in some cases by simply turning the tent round, so as to make the tent-door face in the opposite direction. This was a definite dismissal ; and the husband entered no more.[1] Similar customs are related of certain North American tribes.

Separation of husband and wife with consequent dissolution of the marriage is in many places quite an ordinary incident. In the Marshall Islands, husband and wife usually separate after a longer or shorter time.[2] On Yap, one of the Pelew Islands, there is hardly a pair of middle age who have not been divorced, though it is constantly observed that after various conjugal changes in the meantime they ultimately return to one another.[3] But easy as divorce is here, and without special formalities, some cause, however trivial, must be alleged. It is not difficult to find such a cause. Adultery, as defined by Yap law, barrenness, or even impertinence by the wife to her husband's mother is enough.[4] The payment of a bride-price,

[1] Robertson Smith, " Kinship," 64, 65.
[2] Steinmetz, " Rechtsverhältnisse," 432, 433.
[3] A. Senfft, " Globus," XCI, 141.   [4] *Ibid.*, 142.

necessitating repayment by the wife's kin on divorce by the husband for the fault of the wife, or the forfeiture by the husband of all claim to it for divorce without sufficient cause, is often a great hindrance to divorce in the lower culture. But no bride-price is paid on Yap; hence dissolution of marriage is facilitated.[1] A Malagasy proverb compares marriage to a knot so lightly tied that it can be undone with the slightest touch.[2] It rests with the Malagasy husband to undo it, though in certain circumstances the wife can practically compel divorce. The husband is not bound to faithfulness to his wife. He, however, generally consults his first wife before taking a second; but if she refuse her consent it is a ground of divorce.[3]

Generally it may be said that the husband, if on a social equality with his wife, is not among the lower races compelled to conjugal fidelity, as the wife most frequently is supposed to be. And where the penalty for the wife's unfaithfulness is nominally death, he is in most cases satisfied by personal chastisement or by divorcing her. In some of the Dutch East Indian islands divorce, formerly unknown, has been introduced in place of the original penalty, death, to which a civilized government was unaccountably opposed.

Almost as various as the conditions of separation (or what we call divorce) are the forms to be observed. Often there are none : the pair simply cease to cohabit, or where the husband is a mere visitor he ceases to call, and both parties seek other mates. Among the Khasis of Assam, separation is occasioned by a variety

---

[1] *Ibid.*, 141.   [2] Sibree, 250.
[3] *Ibid.*, 253, 254 ; Ellis, " Madagascar," I, 168, 172.

of causes, such as adultery, barrenness, incompatibility
of temperament ; or it may come about simply by
agreement. But a ceremony which must be witnessed
by some acquaintances and friends, as well as the
relatives on both sides, is performed by an exchange of
cowries or small coins, which the husband finally throws
on the ground. A crier is then sent round the village
to proclaim the divorce, saying in so many words :
" Hear, O villagers, that U. and K. have become
separated in the presence of the elders. Hei ! thou,
O young man, canst go and make love to K., for she is
now unmarried ; and thou, O spinster, canst make love
to U. Hei ! there is no let or hindrance from henceforth."[1] The Musquakie Indians of North America
are wont to allow a married pair who cannot agree
to separate. But they must first go hand-in-hand to the
head chief's council, where the one who first suggested
parting asks for a divorce. A counsellor hands from
a bundle kept ready for the purpose a dry twig to the
petitioner. He (or she) hands it to the unsatisfactory
mate, who breaks it and drops the fragments on the
ground. From that moment both the man and the
woman are free to marry again, and sometimes do so.
No one loses caste by reason of a divorce, but unlike a
maiden there is no long and romantic courtship for a
divorced woman, any more than for a widow.[2] The
Barée-speaking Toradjas of Mid-Celebes allow divorce,
but it must take place in public, just as the marriage
has taken place in public. When the village elders have
tried in vain to heal the quarrel, and failing this have
assessed the rights and wrongs of the parties, their

[1] Gurdon, " Khasis," 79, 80.
[2] Miss Owen, " F. L. Musquakie Indians," 146.

relations henceforth to the children, and the compensation, of any, to be paid on either side, a length of rattan is halved in two and each party keeps a portion. Or, with some tribes, it is a coco-nut that is cut in two, and one piece given with a lemon to each party. This formal proceeding is looked upon as very solemn, as a sort of oath, and not to be omitted. The husband cannot afterwards wed the same woman again ; or if he does he must pay a new bride-price, and a fine into the bargain.[1] It is needless further to illustrate the diversity of ceremony required for a divorce.

We go on to consider the rights of the child. Infanticide is largely practised in the lower culture, both in the shape of abortion and of murder after birth. The conditions of savage life are such that it is impossible for a woman who has to follow the wanderings of the tribe and to contribute materially by her labour to the sustenance of the family, to rear more than one or two young children who are still of an age to depend upon her care. She is compelled to suckle them for much longer than is necessary under civilized conditions, and the attempt to feed them with other food leads to malnutrition with its sequel in disease and frequently death. The testimony to this cause of infanticide is universal, though the reasons given by savages themselves are often superstitious. Naturally, deformed and weakling children are most readily destroyed. Twins and children born in other than the ordinary course, or with other than the ordinary characteristics, are generally condemned. The infant's fate is as a rule decided at birth, before it has had time to obtain a

[1] Adriani en Kruyt, " De Barée-sprekende Toradjas," 34—36.

hold on parental affection. Among the lowest peoples, as the Australian Blackfellows, the decision is usually left to the mother. The Kai of north-eastern New Guinea leave it to the mother and sisters of the woman who has given birth to the child ; no man has anything to say in the matter, which is regarded as a woman's affair.[1] In communities in which the fathers' power is developed it is he who as head of the household determines the question. Among the ancient Norse the child, when born, was laid on the ground. If the father accepted it as his own and decided to rear it he picked it up ; otherwise it was put to death or exposed and abandoned. In Germany, where a similar rite was in use, it was the midwife who by permission of the father picked it up and handed it to him ; hence the German word for midwife (*hebamme*).[2] The custom among the Romans seems to have been the same.[3] As between the two sexes a girl is more usually put to death or exposed than a boy, for in savage conditions a boy is more necessary for the life of the community by the services he will fulfil as hunter and warrior. In India female infanticide has been almost universal, stimulated by the prevalent hypergamy, the custom of striving to marry a daughter in a caste higher than the one in which she is born and the inordinate expense to her father of such a marriage.[4] Among the Bantu of South Africa, on the other hand, where a bride-price,

[1] Neuhauss, " Deutsch Neu Guinea," III, 91.

[2] " Arch. f. Religionswissenschaft," VIII, 7 ; Grinun, " Deutsche Rechtsalterthümer," 455.

[3] Augustine, " De Civ. Dei," IV, 11 ; " Arch. f. Religionswissenschaft," VIII, 6 ; cf. " E. R. E.," art. " Birth, Greek, and Roman."

[4] Gait, " Rep. Census of India, 1911," I, 215–217.

often heavy, must be paid by the bridegroom, girls are more desired than boys.

Where mother-right prevails little distinction is made between legitimate and illegitimate children. In either case they swell the family or the clan of the mother, and such increase is always welcome, provided the means of subsistence are not trenched upon. It is usual, however, if a girl, in the conditions of free access of the unmarried of both sexes which are common, be found pregnant, that efforts are made to get her married to her lover. Under father-right the supervision of sexual relations between the unmarried becomes stricter, because virginity in a bride is prized, and hence attains a greater market value. This leads gradually to the growth of sexual morality, though, owing to the increased value of children there is much difference in this respect : a girl who has already given evidence of her fecundity is the more easily married on that account ; and a husband will even gladly take her " ready-made family " as his own, and they become his legal children. Father-right is generally accompanied by a development of ancestor-worship. A son is therefore required to carry on the ancestral rites, which cannot be done by a stranger. It is his duty not only to perform them himself, but also to procure in his turn a son to continue them after his death. To acquire a son who can be so reckoned, a man will therefore accept as his own his wife's offspring, though he had no part in begetting him.

At or about the age of puberty among the lowest races, and indeed far up in the stages of civilization, a child is required to undergo the puberty ceremonies. In the case of a boy these ceremonies often involve permanent separation from his mother and bring his childhood to an end. He is secluded for the ceremony with male companions of the same age ; they are drilled in endurance and courage by the test of hardships, the traditions and mysteries of the tribe are revealed to them, and they are carefully instructed in the laws and customs which they will have as adults to observe. Amòng many peoples they suffer mutilation, sometimes merely by the knocking out of a tooth, but commonly in the eastern hemisphere by circumcision. The details of the rites are very various, and it is unnecessary to describe them. In Australia, where they have been greatly developed, in Central and South Africa (among the Bantu tribes), and elsewhere, it is usual to perform them upon a number of youths at the same time. In Australia a disciplinary object is prominent to render the novices amenable to the rule of the old men, and so to perpetuate the gerontocracy. Among the Bantu the sexual element in the rites seems to prevail, and they are accordingly followed by a temporary outburst of licentiousness. In North America, on the contrary, the adolescent of an austerer race submits to his experiences alone, with the intent by fasting and penance not merely to prove his powers of endurance, but also to gain for himself the compassion of the higher powers and as hunter and warrior a supernatural helper on whom he can rely amid all difficulties and tribulations.

Girls are subjected at puberty to corresponding rites. On the first appearances of the menses they are everywhere among savage peoples isolated, frequently shut up in the dark and only allowed out of doors in a limited fashion by night and compelled to observe a number of other prohibitions, including a severe restriction of the quantity and quality of their food, though the opposite course is adopted in West Africa of fattening them by stuffing them with food in the " paint-house " in which they are incarcerated. This retirement is enforced among different tribes for varying periods, from a few days to months and even years. The Bantu of Central and South Africa, in addition, collect them in " schools," similar to those of the boys, where they are put through a like course of testing and instruction. They are then ready for sexual intercourse, often anticipated among those voluptuous peoples, and for marriage. Before marriage is allowed by the Arunta and their neighbours in Central Australia girls are obliged to submit to rites of mutilation as cruel and senseless as those of the boys.[1] There, and in other places, notably in the north of New Guinea among the Bánaro, the puberty and marriage rites are celebrated at one and the same time and are indistinguishable.[2]

Thus, for a girl, marriage is the symbol and equivalent of adult life. A boy, however, who has passed through the puberty rites does not always attain complete emancipation and equality as adult, until after further trials and submission to his elders. Thus the Australian youth has still to submit to many restrictions, especially of food, from which he is only gradually released. Among many peoples, before a youth is recognized as a man, and in any case before it is possible for him to marry, he must give undoubted proofs of his valour and his success in hunting. In the East Indian

---

[1] Spencer and Gillen, " Central Tribes," 93 ; " Northern Tribes," 134.

[2] Thurnwald, " Mem. Amer. Anthrop. Assocn.," III, 260.

islands, where head-hunting is practised, he must bring home a human head. In North America a lover must lay at his sweetheart's door substantial products of the chase, ere he is successful in his suit.

In adult life, too, everyone finds himself fenced round with restrictions. That the life of a savage is a life of freedom has repeatedly been shown to be a mistake. In truth there is no life more closely bound in fetters which hamper or absolutely preclude movement in any direction. He must do what his fathers have been accustomed to do, and nothing else. Law and precedent bind him hand and foot. An experienced and able missionary writes of the Bantu native of the Congo Basin : " He has a wonderful power of imitation, but he lacks invention and initiative ; but this lack is undoubtedly due to the suppression of the inventive faculty. For generations it has been the custom to charge with witchcraft anyone who has commenced a new industry or discovered a new article of barter. The making of anything out of the ordinary has brought on the maker a charge of witchcraft that again and again has resulted in death by the ordeal. To know more than others, to be more skilful than others, more energetic, more acute in business, more smart in dress has often caused a charge of witchcraft and death. Therefore the native, to save his life and live in peace, has smothered his inventive faculty and all spirit of enterprise has been driven out of him."[1] Not less emphatic are Messrs. Spencer and Gillen of the Central Australians : " As amongst all savage tribes, the Australian native is bound hand and foot by custom. What his forefathers did before him—that he must

[1] Weeks, " Among Congo Cannibals," 177.

do. If during the performance of a ceremony his ancestors painted a white line across the forehead, that line he must paint. Any infringement of custom, within certain limitations, is visited with sure and often severe punishment."[1]

Most interesting of the innumerable rules thus binding one in the lower culture is the observance of prohibitions which to our mind have no logical ground. That is, however, because we reason on totally different lines from the " primitive " man. Not merely is the ignorance of the " primitive " very great, it is bounded only by his immediate surroundings ; and these are surveyed through the medium only of his needs, his fears, his desires, and his hopes. They thus remain completely enveloped and tinted by an emotional atmosphere, of which they cannot be divested. He is unable to regard them dispassionately, objectively. Unused to analysis, he cannot distinguish the facts from his own feelings concerning them. Limited as his knowledge is, the fear of the unknown is apt to prevail in all his perceptions. Instinctively he takes precautions ; and these precautions, handed down through generations, harden into habits, into unreasoning superstitions. There is no individual thought, his emotions are collective, and—as collective emotions always are—are emphasized until they become an obsession. Under these influences prohibitions and rules of procedure are evolved that a cool onlooker, such as the savage cannot be, sees to be unnecessary, useless, absurd. Acts are to be avoided, or on the other hand to be done, under mysterious penalties. Since, from his ignorance, the savage draws no line

[1] Spencer and Gillen, " Central Tribes," 11.

between the natural and the supernatural, or rather everything is equally natural to him, mysteries are a part of his daily life. Magic is a matter of course ; it is—at least in the early stages—indistinguishable from religion, only gradually becomes separated and never completely so ; though he learns to draw a line between magic performed for the general good and anti-social magic. The one he approves and practises ; the other he reprobates and punishes. The very means by which he protects himself from anti-social magic are what we should call magical—amulets, mystical rules and prohibitions. These avail not only against human witchcraft (or anti-social magic), but also against the mysterious beings—spirits, gods, demons—and vague influences by which he deems himself surrounded.

Prohibitions of the kind referred to are generally known as taboos. The word taboo is Polynesian— *tabu* or *tapu*—meaning set apart by way either of sanctity or of pollution. It has been adopted into English and other civilized languages to express a prohibition or restriction fortified by a mysterious sanction, such as is commonly found to bind peoples in the lower culture, and in a secondary and looser sense as a shunning or prohibition by society of a person or an act or line of conduct generally reprobated or disliked. Though found everywhere among primitive communities it is most influential in Polynesia and Melanesia, where it has been developed into a great engine of government. In New Zealand, for example, every chief was surrounded by taboos. The sacredness of which I have already spoken was derived from his ancestors and his priestly functions in relation to them ;

and it extended to everything belonging to him or coming in contact with him. It was in fact an attribute or manifestation of ghostly power, the greater in proportion to his descent and his earthly might : temporal and spiritual power being often confused, or the former being held to imply the latter. No one, therefore, could touch him or anything belonging to him ; his house was *tapu* and no one could eat in it or light his pipe from the fire, else the persons who did so would die. On the other hand, if he himself touched anything belonging to another person, or even if a drop of his blood fell upon it, it became instantly *tapu* to him, and its previous owner lost it. The applications of this principle were endless in number. Among other instances it is related that a chief lost his tinder-box. Several persons successively found it and lit their pipes from it. But when they learned to whom it belonged they literally died of fright.[1] A missionary once found a chief choking with a fish-bone in his throat, and none of his followers dared to assist him, because it would have been necessary to touch his head (his most sacred part). The missionary boldly (with the aid of a pair of scissors) extracted the bone, and thus saved the chief's life. But when the latter had recovered his speech his first words were—not thanks for the service thus rendered to him, but a command to his followers to seize the scissors as a payment for having touched his sacred throat.[2]

Another application of the principle of taboo is that of the taboo-sign, by which plantations and fruit trees are protected from thieves. These signs are suspended

---

[1] Taylor, " Te-ika-a-Mani," 164 *sqq.*
[2] *Ibid*, 518.

from, or affixed to, the objects to be protected ; they are a symbolic claim by the owner, a prohibition to all and sundry to interfere with the object, and a conditional curse on the transgressor. Coco-nut leaflets plaited in the form of a sea-pike and suspended from the trees to be protected would prevent a would-be thief from touching the fruit, lest the next time he went to sea he should be mortally wounded by a fish of the kind. Other signs denounce similar fates as a penalty for breach of the owner's rights ; and they are said to be most effective guardians.[1] Such taboo-signs are not by any means confined to Polynesia.

Many taboos are social or ritual in origin and intention. Thus among the Ifugao of Luzon it is taboo for persons of other districts to pass through a rice-field while it is being harvested ; and indulgence in verbal abuse, indelicate language, or reference to sexual matters, and the commission of certain acts, are prohibited in the presence of relatives of the opposite sex with whom marriage is forbidden. The infraction of this taboo is a serious offence.[2] In Assam, among the Naga tribes of Manipur, it is customary for a village to celebrate what is called a *genna* (prohibition or taboo) on various occasions, periodical or extraordinary, in the course of which certain rites are performed. At these times every one is compelled to abstain from labour, and the village is closed against all entrance by persons outside and all exit by persons from within. Moreover, certain foods and drink are prohibited. The genna lasts for several days, sometimes as many as ten. The custom

[1] Turner, " Nineteen Years in Polynesia," 294.
[2] Barton, " Univ. Coll. Sub.," XV, 12.

is not confined to Assam, but is known over a considerable area, as far even as the Philippine Islands.[1] Again, it is forbidden by many peoples to mention the names of their gods, or of the dead, especially the recently dead, or even one's own name or the names of other living persons. The supreme god of the Chinese is referred to as *Tien*, Heaven, a circumlocution which we ourselves often make use of.[2] Similarly, the Berbers of Southern Morocco, in speaking of the *jinn* in the afternoon or evening, when the use of their name is prohibited, refer to them as " those others," " those unseen," or by equivalent phrases, just as the Irish peasantry speak of the fairies as " the gentry " or in some such way.[3] The Egyptian gods had secret names, as the Hindu gods have to the present day, and nobody dares to make use of them, The Kiowa of North America drop from the language any word which suggests the name of a person lately deceased, and substitute for it another word : a custom which introduces a considerable difficulty in tracing the philological connexion of words and the comparison with presumably related tongues.[4] A like custom is found among many other peoples in the lower culture, notably among the southern Bantu.[5] In Greenland the Eskimo will not pronounce their own names. It is needless to illustrate further a prohibition known in one form or other all over the world in the lower culture.[6]

[1] Hodson, " Naga Tribes," 164 *sqq.* ; Barton, *loc. cit.*
[2] Legge, " Religions of China," 8 ; Hilderic Friend, " F. L. Record," IV, 76, citing Edkins.
[3] Westermarck, " Moral Ideas," II, 640.
[4] " Rep. Bur. Ethn.," XVII, 152, 231.
[5] Leslie, " Among the Zulus," 173 ; Shooter, 221.
[6] Rasmussen, 10.

Every ancient code of law, not excepting the Mosaic legislation, comprises social and ritual prohibitions and regulations of the kinds just referred to ; and they are apparently placed on equal footing with the moral commands of the code. Taboos of one kind or another are in fact taboos universally observed. They are often so ancient that their origin and meaning are undiscoverable, they are rooted in the fear of the unknown ; and, as Dr. Marett has pointed out, they do constitute a defence against the magical or mysterious powers imputed by tribes and societies of men to their surroundings, whether natural or what we call supernatural. The observance of the taboos of any community is as much a duty to oneself and to the community as that of any positive command concerning the mutual relations of members of the community ; for the breach of these taboos may entail great and unexpected evils, not only on the breaker but involving the whole community of which he is a part.

CHAPTER IV

PROPERTY. OWNERSHIP. INHERITANCE.
BARTER. MONEY

IN the earliest stages of civilization now discoverable mankind is possessed of no individual property beyond the scanty clothing, the miserable ornaments, the weapons, and the few utensils in daily use. All other property known to tribes in this condition is held in common by the community. Even the products of the chase by which they live are not regarded as solely the property of the successful hunter, but are shared with other members of the community. How far the right to share has extended varies among different peoples. Possibly it originally included all members of the community. Of the inhabitants of Namaqualand (Hottentots, a pastoral people) it is recorded that " when a family kill a sheep they only obtain a share of it, as the neighbours, who all know what has been done, repair to the house and the whole is eaten up before they leave it. This," we are told, " seems from custom to be a kind of law among them, which it would be difficult for a family to set aside."[1]

[1] J. Campbell, " Travels," 1815, 303. In another edition dated in the same year, 420.

The Hottentots, however, are not on the lowest step of civilization ; and whatever may be the cause of such extensive rights to share food among them, hunting tribes have generally limited these rights. The Veddas of Ceylon, a very lowly race of aborigines, recognize greater claims on the part of certain relatives than of other members of the community. Dr. and Mrs. Seligman report that " every Vedda so readily helps all other members of the community, and shares any game he may kill or honey he may take in so liberal a manner, that at first it was difficult to determine who were the individuals who had a special claim on others of the group. Certainly at first sight it seemed as if all game were equally divided among the members of the group ; but after a little time we perceived that, while an unmarried man looked especially after his mother, a married man's father-in-law had at least an equal claim on his son-in-law, and in practice often received more attention, since a man generally spent most of his time with his wife's family." Accordingly the wife's father usually receives the largest share of all game killed by his daughter's husband.[1] Very similar rules are observed by the Australian Black-fellows.

The Oraons of Chota Nagpur have an annual Great Summer Hunt when the various villages send out their quota of men. The game is equally divided between all the villages which have joined the hunt. On their return, " when the hunters from each village approach the limits of their village, they subdivide their division of game into as many shares as there are families of Oraons in the village. Even families whose members

[1] Seligman, " Veddas," 66.

consist of only women and old men and children who could not take part in the hunt are given their respective shares."[1] This seems a ceremonial recognition of ancient rights. On the ordinary, less formal occasions the game is divided among the members of the party only. " The man who actually bagged the game gets two shares, one for having killed the animal and another as a villager and a member of the party." [2] Even here there seems a relic of communal right. So, too, among the Teu'a of North America, where the distribution is limited to those who have taken part in the hunt. " The Teu'a hunt is conducted on communistic principles. In a band of hunters it is never the one who killed a piece of large game who gets it ; he generally receives but an insignificant share, or none at all. By common agreement it is distributed among the party, or given whole to one who then is expected to cook it and serve it as a banquet to the whole village." [3]

On the other hand, the traditions of the Yakuts (like the Hottentots, a pastoral people) point to the continuity—at least, so long as they kept droves of horses—of distribution to all the kin on the slaughter of an animal. The kin would be the only neighbours, and they probably had an interest in the drove. It is therefore surmised that the custom had its origin in distribution to a body of persons who had a right to share in the products of the drove.[4] How far this applies to the Hottentots is a question which we have no direct means of determining, since they had passed the stage

---

[1] Roy, " Oraons," 236.
[2] *Ibid.*, 157.
[3] J. Jetté, " J. R. A. I.," XXXIX, 483.
[4] Sumner, *ibid.*, XXXI, 68.

of common ownership when Kolben, at the beginning of the eighteenth century, wrote his elaborate account of them. It may be observed, however, that, though the ownership of herds was not then in common, the cattle of a kraal still ran all together, and the poorest inhabitant, who had only a single sheep, had the privilege of turning it into the flock, where it was tended and taken as much care of, though he was not present, as the sheep of the richest and most powerful; and that all the men of the kraal took turns in performing the duties of herdsmen or shepherds. This points to the joint ownership of the herds, and the distribution may well have been only to persons who had a right as joint-owners to participate.[1]

The articles of personal ownership—clothing, weapons, ornaments, and implements—are so constantly associated with the person to whom they belong, that they are hardly thought of apart from him. In the processes of native thought they become identified with him. Any use by others is likely to be dangerous to him, and magic to his detriment may be wrought through their medium. Their ownership and use are therefore jealously guarded. When he dies they are buried with him, not necessarily as being useful to him in that life after death in which most savages believe, but as being his—things to which he has an indefeasible claim, which are in fact thought of as an extension of his personality. Thus the Yahgans of Tierra del Fuego split the dead man's canoe in twain and destroy all his belongings.[2] The Buandik of South

[1] Kolben, 168.
[2] " Proc. Cong. Americanists, 1915," 427. Mrs. James Smith, " Booandik Tribe," 9.

Australia burn all that he owned, " so that nothing shall be left to revive the sorrow of the relatives," and the dead are thus utterly forgotten. In both these cases the effects are destroyed to put an end to the memory and the sorrow of the survivors. In a higher degree of civilization the Melanesians of Florida, one of the Solomon Islands, hang up the arms of the deceased on his hut and leave them and the hut to fall into decay. " These things," says Bishop Codrington, " are not set up that they may in a ghostly manner accompany their former owner ; they are set there for a memorial of him as a great and valued man. . . . With the same feeling they cut down the dead man's fruit-trees as a mark of respect and affection, not with any notion of these things serving him in the world of ghosts ; he ate of them, they say, when alive, he will never eat again, and no one else shall have them."[1]

This is a practice common not only in Melanesia but also in the East Indian Archipelago. In South America it is widely spread. The Yaguas, to mention only one example, destroy at a relative's death his whole property, indeed, everything that he has touched. His domesticated animals are killed and his plantation demolished. If a child die, his father and mother put his weapons and ornaments with him in the grave.[2] Nor is the practice of destroying the personal belongings of a dead man confined to the southern hemisphere. It is recorded of North American tribes and of Negro tribes. It seems to have been by no means unknown to the early Greeks. It is a funeral custom among the gipsies

[1] Codrington, 255 ; see also *ibid.*, 263.
[2] Int. Arch., XIII, Suppl. 57.

of this country to the present day ; [1] and relics are perhaps found in the department of Ille et Vilaine, Brittany, in the belief that everything that has belonged to a dead man will speedily disappear : his clothes, whatever may be done to preserve them, will be promptly moth-eaten, his cattle will die by accident or disease, if they are not sold to the butchers by those who come after him. [2]

As, however, in the course of civilization property is accumulated and its value as a means of acquiring power is found out, new reasons are discovered for the custom of destroying the property of the deceased or burying it with him. It will be useful to him in the spirit world, either to propitiate the rulers there or for his own use. And, on the other hand, the desire of the survivors to retain it for themselves in this world grows stronger. This results in the reduction to a minimum of the goods thus sacrificed, until they are only the least valuable of his possessions—a mere symbol of the intention. In another way, too, the symbolism is effected : the corpse is decked out with all the valuables of the deceased, but they are carefully removed before burial or cremation. The natives of the Trobriand Islands to the east of New Guinea explain the practice by saying that, as the ghost of the man goes away to the region of the departed but the corpse remains, so the ghosts of the jewels and axe-blades with which the corpse had been adorned go away though the objects themselves remain. [3] Finally, of course, in the highest civilizations all pretence of

---

[1] " F. L.," XXIV, 239, 348, 352.
[2] Orain, " F. L. L'Ille et Vilaine," II, 299.
[3] Malinowsky, " J. R. A. I.," XLVI, 359.

yielding up the property of the deceased is abandoned, all attempts to identify his personality with his valuables are forgone, and they remain to be divided according to rule or the will of the defunct, lawfully expressed, among his relatives.

Fruit-trees may seem strange objects to be reckoned among a man's personal belongings. According to our law they are inseparable from the land on which they stand—they are part of the realty, as we say. This, however, is not the law in Melanesia. There they are treated as something separable : the land and the trees upon it are independent objects of property. The land may be owned by one man and the trees by another ; though in Fiji the property in the trees " is rather in the fruit than in the tree, and is therefore not considered to be in the land. You may take the fruit, but you must not cut down the tree without the owner's permission."[1] This approximation to civilized law is interesting. Where fruit-trees are distinguished from the soil in which they are rooted it is not surprising to find the house treated in the same way. Among the lowest savages the camp is so often changed, it is so fugitive, if one may be allowed the expression, sometimes consisting of a few improvised wind-screens only, that it is of no importance : it does not exist long enough, nor is it individual enough to be distinctive of its owner. In such cases the whole camp is usually abandoned : a not infrequent consequence of a death in lower culture, probably arising from fear of the ghost or of ceremonial pollution. This is a frequent cause for the removal even of whole villages where the buildings are comparatively substantial. Elsewhere the

[1] Codrington, 61 (citing Rev. L. Fison), 62, 65, 68.

corpse is buried or abandoned in the hut, and the hut is sometimes destroyed. A relic of this is found among the Cheremiss, a people of Finnish affinities in the south of Russia. They no longer deposit the corpse in the hut and leave it there in peace ; but, when it is brought out in its coffin and placed upon the wagon which is to convey it to the burial-ground with its belongings, the family in bidding the deceased farewell pray him not to take his house away with him, but to leave it to his heirs.[1] It is impossible to discuss here fully the destruction of property that takes place in primitive communities on the occasion of a death. I only want to point out that whatever other causes there may be in the fear of the ghost, or of witchcraft, or ceremonial pollution, there is one cause of very archaic origin which gives weight and persistence to the others, namely, the primitive extension of the idea of a man's personality to all the objects commonly associated with him in his lifetime.

Land, however, is property of a totally different kind. It is impossible to identify it with the personality of any individual. A community of roving hunters seeking their food from game, or from wild fruits and seeds (and this is a stage that science does not enable us to get behind), rarely travels beyond the district with which its members are familiar, unless driven by want of supplies or some other special cause. That district may be wide ; but, however wide, it has boundaries hardly recognizable to us but well known to the community. Within those boundaries it is looked upon by the community as its own territory. It resents the intrusion, without permission, of members of any other

[1] Smirnov, I, 137.

community upon it. At this stage, and for long afterwards, no individual is regarded as the exclusive owner
of any part of it. This is the position of the Australian
natives. Our information does not enable us to say
how far, if at all, it is shared by the Bushmen of South
Africa in reference to the vast regions over which they
once wandered undisturbed. As little do we know of
the Pygmies of the Central African forests, who perhaps
have hardly arrived at the notion of claiming exclusive
rights in their habitat. But speaking of hunting tribes
generally, it seems that such exclusive rights are claimed
first for the whole tribe or a division of it, and that
from this the notion of ownership of land has been
gradually developed with increasing civilization. The
starting-point, however, has been a claim, not so much
to the land itself, as of a right for the members of the
community, or group, to hunt unhindered over any
part of the territory, to take and appropriate the game
and the products of the soil found upon it, and to hold
assemblies and perform ceremonies at the accustomed
spots within its limits. There is no inheritance of land,
or of these rights, because the community is (to adapt
a legal term of much later date) a quasi-corporation
that never dies. With increase of numbers or growing
complexity of organization the land of the community,
or group, may be parcelled out, so as to allot to a clan
(in cases where the members of a clan dwell adjacently)
or a family, or other subdivision, a definite portion
over which they may exercise these rights exclusively,
as seems to be the case in some parts of Australia.[1]

Thus in a somewhat higher stage of civilization than

[1] " J. A. I.," VII, 291 ; XIII, 278 ; " J. R. A. I.," XLIII,
146, 147.

that of the Australian natives, where the population was settled but agriculture was as yet undeveloped, the Maori of New Zealand held land primarily by tribal right ; but within this tribal right each free warrior of the tribe had particular rights over some portion. He could not part with the land, because it was not his to give or sell ; but he had better rights to certain portions than others of his tribe. He would claim by having the bones of his father or grandfather there, or if they once rested there ; or by the fact of his navel-string having been cut there ; or by his blood having been shed on it ; or by having been cursed there ; or by having helped in the war party which took the land ; or by his wife being owner by descent ; or by having been invited by the owners to live there.[1] These very various, and to us strange, titles are derived mainly from ancestor-worship or from taboo—ideas and customs which formed the basis of Polynesian culture. In the extreme north-east of Asia the Yakuts, an entirely pastoral people, knew nothing of private property in lands, not even in the house. Communism was the essence of their policy, which we have already described. To maintain this communism in accordance with the varying needs of their herds of horses the land of a tribe needed to be re-allotted among the *naslegs*, and that of the *naslegs* among the *sibs* from time to time. This was done by officers specially appointed in public assembly, and no individual property was recognized, or any immunity of the property of *nasleg* or *sib* from the law of redistribution.[2] In these circumstances all progress was debarred. An exclusively

[1] E. Tregear, " J. A. I.," XIX, 106.
[2] " J. A. I.," XXXI, 70, 74.

pastoral and communistic policy leads to no advance in civilization.

The advent of agriculture is the beginning of a revolution, which ultimately establishes individual property in land as in other things. It is no part of our business to inquire into the origin of agriculture. Whether introduced from abroad by invaders and conquerors or by some less drastic form of culture-contact, or developed from within, the result is the same : it gives the native a new interest in the land, a new use, which ensures a more tenacious hold of it as the cultivation of the soil becomes more and more the chief means of livelihood to the people.

Individual property in land, however, is of slow growth. This may be illustrated from the Mundas and Oraons, two aboriginal tribes of Chota-Nagpur in Central India. Among the former the village community owns all the lands within the village area. Separate fields, it is true, of the lands brought under cultivation are cultivated by individual Mundas for their own profit ; but the proprietary rights belong to the corporate body of the Mundari inhabitants of the village, and the consent of all those joint owners must be obtained for the transfer of any land. Among the Oraons, on the other hand, the joint ownership of the corporate body of the villagers extends only to the jungle and other unoccupied lands ; or, rather, it did so extend until comparatively recent times, for the rights of the community have been distorted and over-ridden by repeated conquests by foreign powers and consequent claims to alien ownership. The result is that among both the Mundas and Oraons the rights of the village are subject to the claims of the paramount landlord, who exercises his rights through an official appointed by him from among the villagers themselves. The rights of the Oraon village community, whatever may be the case of those of the Mundas, over the unoccupied lands have further dwindled to rights to jungle trees and jungle produce, rights of pasturage and of reclaiming waste lands, and can only be exercised under certain restrictions. The cultivated lands, however, are vested, subject only, perhaps, to the claims of the superior landlord (which may be little more than nominal), in the family of the cultivator. This, again, is a species of corporate ownership, resting on the rule that the members of a family dwell together and work together in the fields held by the head of the family. When the head of a family dies the ownership remains in the family, represented by the succeeding head.[1]

The development of individual property in land is seriously retarded by the nature of primitive agriculture. The forest must be cleared and the land prepared, both works involving the co-operation of many hands. As systematic manuring is unknown, the land becomes exhausted in a few seasons, and is abandoned and fresh ground broken up. This often means the abandonment of the entire settlement and removal to a different site. Such a change causes little difficulty to communities in an early stage of culture. Indeed it is familiar. The dwellings are of perishable materials, easily obtained, and liable to be frequently renewed, or, from various causes other than exhaustion of the neighbouring soil, such as a death, or an epidemic,

[1] Roy, "Oraons," 116–119; Risley, "T. C. Bengal," II; "Ethnographic Glossary," 105–107, 149.

removed to another site. Thus in the basin of the Upper Amazon, where the community resides in a single large house, individual tribesmen may build separate small dwellings for themselves and their families in the bush, without relinquishing their right to a corner in the common house. And they often cultivate individual patches of plantation near their individual dwellings, while the main plantation is adjacent to the common house, and the greater part of it is assigned to the chief, because not only has he greater labour at command, but his produce is, partly at all events, expended on the common wants. All these plantations are abandoned every few years because of the exhaustion of the soil, conflicts with other tribes, or some other reason. In such circumstances nobody can hold or retain separate property in land, except while he is actually occupying or cultivating it.[1] Among the Iroquois of North America, a mainly agricultural society, the land was vested in the clan, the house was vested in the family or division of the clan occupying it. This was facilitated by the matrilineal practice of the tribe, in accordance with which the husband went to live in the house of the wife's family. "Each individual," says Morgan, "can improve and enclose any portion of their common domain, and sell or retain such improvements, in the same manner as with personal property; but they have no power to transfer the title to the land to each other or to strangers." [2] In short, the land only belonged to an individual or a family so long as it was actually occupied or cultivated by the claimant.

[1] Whiffen, 41, 47, 102 *sqq.*, 161.
[2] Morgan, " League," I, 317 ; II, 118, 272.

The impulse to exclusive ownership (not necessarily individual ownership) is often found in the difficulties to be overcome in the cultivation of land. Thus, to select only one illustration out of many that might be given, the Ifugaos of Luzon, who cultivate rice on their mountain-sides, have found it necessary to terrace and irrigate extensively. " On these steep mountains that rise from sea-level to heights of six to eight thousand feet—mountains as steep probably as any in the world —there have been carved out, with wooden spades and wooden crowbars, terraces that run like the crude but picturesque ' stairsteps ' of a race of giants, from the bases almost to the summits. Some of these terrace-walls are fifty feet high. More than half are walled with stone. Water to flood these terraces is retained by a little rim of earth at the outer margin. The soil is turned with a wooden spade in preparation for planting. No mountain is too steep to be terraced, if it afford an unfailing supply of water for irrigation." [1] Accordingly, the subjects of so much strenuous labour are permanently owned either by a family or an individual on its behalf ; and the community seems to have no claim upon them. " Family properties consist of rice-lands, forest-lands, and heirlooms. The Ifugao attitude is that lands and articles of value that have been handed down from generation to generation cannot be the property of any individual. Present holders possess only a transient and fleeting possession, or, better, occupation, insignificant in duration in comparison with the decades, and perhaps centuries, that have usually elapsed since the field or heirloom came into the possession of the family. Their possession

[1] Barton, " Univ. Cal. Pub.," XV, 9.

is more of the nature of a trust than an absolute ownership—a holding in trust for future generations." Yet
family property may in case of necessity be sold after
consultation with the kin, by means of complex ceremonies in which the near kin of both buyer and seller
take part. Side by side with this family property there
are things which are individual property. In addition
to objects of personal use, such as those discussed on a
previous page, houses, valuable trees, and sweet-
potato fields, are so reckoned. "Dwellings are movable
property in Ifugao. A man, with the aid of his kinsmen can, and frequently does, take a house to pieces,
move it to a different site, and set it up again before
sunset. The plot on which a house stands, has no
value," and is presumably abandoned. Coco-nut
trees, coffee-trees and areca palms, are individual
property, and can be transferred from person to person
apart from the land on which they stand. Sweet-
potato fields are clearings on the mountain-sides about
the village. But their value is only passing ; they
quickly lose their fertility, and are abandoned in from
two to six years. After abandonment the field slowly
regains its fertility. Then the first person who begins
clearing it again becomes its temporary possessor,
until he in his turn abandons it. Such fields are seldom
the subject of sales, though the crop, with temporary
possession for the purpose of ingathering, may be disposed of. Abandonment of rice-land and forest-land,
on the other hand, does not mean relinquishment of
ownership. The owner may recover possession at any
time, subject to his paying anyone who has taken
possession in the meantime for his expenditure of labour
upon a rice-field, or if he has had possession for the

same number of years that it lay abandoned, without
any payment. Forest-lands divested of their wood
by the owner may be planted with sweet-potatoes by
anyone. The owner must inform him at once
if he object, otherwise he will, before obtaining
possession again, be required to pay for the
labour or allow the harvesting of one crop from the
land.[1]

Now the land defined as family property requires
much labour to reduce and keep it under cultivation,
and to fell and remove the timber; and the careful and
prolonged co-operation of many hands is needed. This
is given by the kinsmen who are to share in the profits
of their toil. The greater the labour, the more tena-
ciously they will hold to the property, and the less
willingly they will see it pass by way of redistribution
into the possession of others. It is not surprising,
therefore, that exclusive ownership of the family has
developed. The objects spoken of by our authority
as "heirlooms" are likewise valuable. They are
personal ornaments of gold, agates, blood-stones and
glass beads, gongs, and rice-wine jars. If not acquired
by the labour and contributions of, they are at least
enjoyed by, all the family. "These articles," we are
told, "are used fully as much by the owner's kin as by
the owner himself; for they wear the beads and ornaments, play the gongs in feasts, and brew rice-wines in
the jars." Heirlooms, of course, these things are not;
they are family property, the enjoyment of which is
shared by all the kin. In this they differ from articles
of individual use and identified with individuals, and
they are assimilated with the land on which the family

[1] Barton, " Univ. Cal. Pub.," XV, 39–44.

labour has been bestowed, and the fruits of which are employed for the maintenance and prosperity of the family under the direction of the holder for the time being.[1]

It may be laid down that the transition from the common ownership of land by a whole community (tribe or clan) to individual ownership has generally been made by way of family ownership, and is based on its reduction under cultivation. Thus in Fiji each village community has its own lands, which are of three kinds : the *yavu* or town-lot, the *gele* or arable land, and the *veikan* or forest. The forest-lands are common to all the real or imputed descendants of the original settlers of the village, all of whom have the right of felling timber for building and other purposes. The town-lots are divided among these descendants, and subdivided until each "family or household" has its own lot, upon which the family dwelling is erected. Between the town-lot and the arable land there is a close connexion, and to establish the ownership of the one appears to go far to establishing the ownership of the other. The arable land is not always, like the town-lots, divided among the various households. Sometimes it is, but sometimes it is not; and in this case there appears to be joint use by all the descendants of the original settlers.[2] "Each generation has the usufruct only, and cannot alienate the land."[3] In other parts of Melanesia there is no appropriation to a village of the bush-land surrounding it. This land is simply waste which anyone is at liberty to reclaim,

[1] *Ibid.*, 40.
[2] L. Fison, " J. A. I.," X, 336 *sqq*.
[3] Codrington, 60 n.

and it thereupon becomes his own. The town-lands, and the cultivated lands are held by individuals, not, however, for their own benefit. The individual holds possession for his lifetime only, and uses what he has inherited as part of the whole property that belongs to his family. There is thus no individual property in land, except what a man has personally reclaimed from the forest. He may plant fruit-trees on another's land with the latter's acquiescence, and then those trees and their fruits will be his personal belonging as much as pigs which he has bought or reared, or any objects of personal use or ornament. " The chiefs have nowhere more property in the land, or more rights over it than other men," whatever they may have claimed in dealings with Europeans, and whatever power they may tyranically have assumed in dealing with their own tribesmen. The ownership of land thus depends upon its reduction under cultivation either by a man or his ancestors. A man who has himself reclaimed land from the waste may apparently do what he likes with it, and it descends to his own children. The people are in a late stage of mother-right, the family is continued through women only, and the property of the ancestors descends through women, so that the ancestral or family property held by a man does not go after his death to his children, but to his sister's children, or to his nearest of kin through his mother. Whether the property claimed by a man as owner because he has brought it under cultivation will ultimately descend in the same way, when the origin of the claim is forgotten, depends on the continued existence and strength of the matrilineal family. The small beginnings of the agnatic family have been accelerated in growth by the advent of the White Man ; and the holder of family property has even now by native law a right to arrange before his death, that his sons may succeed to a part of it. Thus a way is opened for the transmutation of family to individual ownership.[1]

In Melanesia and Polynesia the chiefs are rather a class than individual monarchs. Where the chieftainship has become a personal dignity the ownership of the lands of the tribe no longer rests directly in the tribe, but in the chief as representing the tribe. Speaking of the Ba-Ronga, a Bantu people of south-east Africa, M. Junod says : " By law the soil belongs to the chief, but only that through him it may become general property. No one can buy land. It is gratuitously assigned to any and all who wish to settle in the country. The mere fact of making submission to the chiefs entitles the native to as much land as may be necessary for his subsistence." The actual allotment is performed by the headmen of the villages, " who obtain the grant of considerable tracts of land which they apportion amongst those under their jurisdiction." They are glad to do this, because the grantee of the land " adds considerably to its value by cultivating an otherwise useless bush," and increases the headman's strength by peopling his tract of country and by making certain payments in labour on the fields the latter retains for his own use.[2] The Ba-Ronga have advanced to descent through the father, and a long way towards individual ownership. The land once granted

---

[1] Codrington, " J. A. I.," XVIII, 311–313. Cf. *ibid.*, " The Melanesians," 59 *sqq.*

[2] Junod, " S. Afr. Tribe," II, 6, 7 ; *ibid.* " Les Ba-Ronga," 186–188.

to a tribesman or settler, it remains his and descends
to his sons, so long as he and they occupy it. If he
quit, he abandons it ; and it then reverts to the common
stock of the chief or headman by whom it was granted.
The wild fruits, if any, on undivided land (there is no
such thing as cultivated fruit) are common property ;
anyone who likes can gather them. The Bantu not
only cultivate the ground ; they are also a pastoral
people. The grazing lands are not divided ; they are
for common use. This system of land tenure is general
throughout the area in South Africa inhabited by the
Bantu.[1]

Farther north, however, the Bangala (also Bantu)
of the Upper Congo, a cannibal tribe who dwell in
towns or villages, each town or village being independent
and consisting of a number of families, but without a
chief recognized by all, have quite a different land-law.
The land surrounding the town belongs to the inhabitants of the town. Within its boundary the people
of the town are free to settle and cultivate any land
not already occupied ; and on the death of the first
cultivator it would be inherited by his children. Between the land of a town and that of the next, a space
of forest-land is neutral ground free to the people of
both towns to hunt, cut timber, and for similar purposes.
In the town the houses appear to belong to individuals.
They only take a day to build, and are easily removed.
When the owner dies he is buried in the house, and it
and any other houses in the row with it (as those built
for his wives adjacent to his own) are abandoned and

---

[1] Junod, " S. Afr. Tribes," 193 ; *ibid*. 15 ; " J. A. I.," XVI, 86 ;
ibid., XIX, 276, 277 ; cf. " Cape Report on Native Laws,"
passim.

left to decay.[1] The Bangala are not a pastoral people.

Thus we have here individual property, the title to which depends on priority of occupation ; and apparently the native, whose sense of time is rudimentary, does not recognize any limit to his right to retrieve possession of land which he has once abandoned, or of which he has been deprived. Statutes of limitation are a weakness of a much more sophisticated stage of civilization.

The Bantu in Uganda erected a military empire, and reached the highest civilization known to any of their race before the coming of the White Man. Their policy was based on the feudal system. The whole of the land belonged to the king. It was held of him by the various chiefs and dignitaries, and they granted it out in portions on condition of the grantees " doing work for them, especially building work, and rendering military service." No sale of land was possible. The clans into which the population was divided indeed possessed their freehold burial-grounds, but they could not sell them to any outsider ; nor could a stranger be buried anywhere in the country without the permission of the king. The men did not themselves cultivate the land they thus held. This was done by the women of the family while the men were occupied in working for the chiefs and the king, or in making bark-cloth in their leisure from this labour. It seems (though I have not found this expressly stated) that the land granted to anyone could be taken back at any time by the king or chief of whom it was held, either at his own caprice or by way of forfeiture for nonfulfilment of

[1] " J. R. A. I.," XXXIX, 109, 424, 426, 429.

the conditions of holding or for crime.[1]   Such a system
is the product of conquest and settlement by invaders
who have established themselves on the spot as a ruling
class :   in this case probably a Hamitic people.   In
Madagascar the rule of the Hovas, originating also in
conquest, has been productive of an even more drastic
result. The Hova sovereigns reduced their subjects
to the condition of slaves : no one could do or have
anything, save in accordance with the sovereign's will.
All land, whether cultivated or uncultivated, belonged
to the sovereign, who could turn out a tenant at a
moment's notice and without any compensation for
improvements or buildings.   On the other hand, the
tenant could do nothing with his land, except to build
or plant, until he had first applied for and received
express permission from the sovereign for the purpose ;
and if the tenant desired to give up, exchange, or
apparently to sell his holding, or to remove elsewhere,
the sovereign might refuse permission.   There is no
military tenure ; but every able-bodied subject not
nominally a slave, or not incapacitated by disease or
inferiority, was obliged to serve in the army, and every
tenant was liable to pay annually the first-fruits of all
crops, as well as a certain quantity of rice in the husk,
together with manual labour, such as preparing the
sovereign's rice-fields (rice being the chief crop), making
roads or embankments, erecting public buildings or
other public works.[2]

The development of a feudal system is only possible
where conquest is accompanied by military settlement
in the midst of a subject population.   In such an event

[1] Roscoe, " Baganda," 268.
[2] G. W. Parker, " J. A. I.," XII, 277.

the leader of the successful invasion develops into a hereditary king, his chiefs of bands receive grants in severalty of tracts of land and become barons and lords, the victorious freemen receive smaller portions while the conquered people sink into serfs on land formerly their own. Where the conquest does not assume this intensive form, the victor is often satisfied to exact a tribute only, leaving the vanquished in actual possession to work out undisturbed in the normal course their problems of land-ownership and civilization, from common ownership by the community, through the narrower circle of the clan or family, to individual ownership. This course is found actually running in India and among the Slavs of Russia and the Balkan peninsula. Historical records and relics in custom and tradition have preserved its memory, or something more than its memory, all over Europe. The claim of the family to share in the benefits of ownership is based on the double bond of blood and of co-operation, all the more effectively rendered since the members, where the family ownership is effective, usually dwell together under a common head. When from any cause they separate, the family property is divided ; and a break-up of the family ultimately leads to ownership in severalty.

The existence of the joint family is directly but little affected by the change of the reckoning of descent from the mother's to the father's side. Where mother-right is in full force, as among the Iroquois or among the Menang Kabau Malays of the Padang Highlands of Sumatra, the family continues to live together and to own and work the family property. When father-right has taken its place the joint family often continues, as in India and Russia, under the headship of the father or, in the event of his death, of brothers succeeding in a definite order ; and the family property vests in the head for the time being for the benefit of the family. The break-up of the family is very slow and gradual. The feeling of solidarity dominates the clan, and with the growth of families within the clan it dominates the family with at least equal strength. This feeling of family solidarity may even subsist after a joint family has ceased to dwell together. Its members may be driven apart by the narrowness of house-room, family quarrels, or other circumstances ; but they may still live in one another's neighbourhood, and they may still put the fruits of their labour into a common stock. In such a case they will not abandon their claim to share in the good things of the family, while, on the other hand, they will continue liable for the crimes and misdeeds of one another, and will be mixed up in the quarrels and lawsuits of the family. This claim and this liability are equal : the one is the measure of the other. The loosing of the family tie thus expressed cannot be done all at once ; it will take generations— centuries if the process be undisturbed, unaccelerated. Conquest, enterprise, individual industry, foreign contact, every incident in the process of civilization loosens it more and more, and tends to set up individualism in its place, until at last individual ownership with its correlative individual responsibility is substituted for family ownership and family liability in the whole circle of rights and duties.

Where this revolution is complete the family as a quasi-corporation no longer exists : inheritance has taken its place. We have already touched on the process of appropriation by the survivors in dealing with articles of personal use. This appropriation naturally occurs earlier with respect to such articles than to the more permanent and less easily divisible land. Even when excuses have been found for not destroying them at the owner's death but keeping them, however, they frequently remain undivided for a certain period and must be purified before being appropriated by the survivors. Thus, the Suk of the East African Protectorate keep the dead man's ornaments and head-dress for a month after his death, and then give them to the official grave-digger of the community, or divide them among the relatives of the deceased. But before so doing the articles in question are purified from their late owner's presence by lustrations of milk.[1] The Ntlakapamux, or Thompson River Indians, of British Columbia burn the lodge in which an adult has died, together with most of his household utensils and the bed on which he has died. Some of his property is placed in or near the grave, and the rest is divided among his relatives. Articles of clothing are also given to be divided among outsiders (not relatives) ; but these before wearing them are careful to wash them, or put them for some time in running water, and afterwards to hang them out for several days. His traps and snares are removed to a distance and hung up in a tree for a long time before being used. His bow and arrows, long leggings, and moccasins no one dares to touch.[2]

Purification, however, cannot apply to land. When individual property in land is established it may be

[1] K. R. Dundas, " J. R. A. I.," XL, 59, 60.
[2] Teit, " Jesup Exped.," I, 331, 332.

subject to the very common rule that a certain time must elapse before it is appropriated. It is then frequently dealt with by means of an elaborate ceremony. The order of succession remains for long undetermined. Sometimes the land under father-right falls to the eldest son. He would have been the head and administrator of the family before individual property was established ; and probably his inheritance is burdened by the maintenance of the women of the family, so long as these are unmarried. Often the inheritance is decided in family conclave, as among the Jekris of West Africa, where, " generally speaking, not the eldest son, but the son adjudged to have most sense (*i.e.* the fittest to succeed) is made heir." It is very common, however, that the dying man expresses his wishes as to the disposal of his property—wishes which are in most cases observed.[1] Here we have the germ of the right of testamentary disposition. The Angámi of the Nágá Hills in the north-east of India possess separate property. Daughters do not, except in certain villages, inherit ; but a property may be left to them by word of mouth. Where they do receive a share of the paternal property, it is not clear from our information whether they receive it on marriage or at the father's death. The sons as they marry receive a share of their father's land, leaving the paternal roof and building houses of their own. In practice the youngest son nearly always inherits his father's house. If at the father's death there be more than one son unmarried, the property is divided between them in equal shares. If a man die leaving no sons the property is as a rule divided among his nearest male relatives. On the

[1] " J. A. I.," XXVIII, 118.

death of a married woman possessed of landed property in her own right, but without children, the rule is the same, unless the property be sold to pay her funeral expenses.[1] The practice of portioning the children as they go out into the world usually results in the youngest being left at home, and consequently inheriting what remains of the paternal estate. It is implied in the parable of the Prodigal Son, and it has in our own country left as a relic the local custom of Borough English (as at Nottingham, Gloucester, and other places), whereby the youngest son of an intestate inherits, to the exclusion of his elder brothers, the real estate situate within the limits to which the custom applies.

It would lead us beyond our space to pursue the various rules of inheritance of landed property. They appear even under matrilineal reckoning of descent, where the sisters or the sisters' children ordinarily succeed to the exclusion of the children of the deceased. But they attain their greatest diversity after the establishment of the patrilineal reckoning ; and they probably follow, as nearly as may be, the lines along which the headship of the family as a quasi-corporation has run, or the lines of division during the period of the gradual break-up of the family, leading to the victory of individualism.

The change in the descent of property from the mother's side to that of the father has often come through slavery. Slavery is an institution which does not arise until a considerable advance is made on archaic savagery. Prisoners are rarely taken in savage warfare. When they are taken, as among many

[1] *Ibid.*, XXVII, 29.

tribes in North America, it is only for the purpose of torturing them to death to gratify the revengful feelings of their captives, or to be adopted into the tribe in place of those who have been killed in the fight, or, lastly, as in Mexico, to be eaten. But as property accumulates, their value as slaves is discovered. In Africa not only prisoners taken in war are enslaved. Men who cannot pay their debts, or their fines, give up to their creditors their children and wives, or in the last result resign themselves as pawns for their liabilities. Though redeemable, this condition frequently results in permanent servitude. Men who get women as pawns, or as slaves, reduce them to concubinage and beget children upon them. These children, though still slaves, may be regarded by their fathers with parental fondness. In such a state of society slavery is not an insupportable condition. Slaves, whether the children of their owners or not, are generally treated as members of the family. It is true they may be liable to be put to death by a callous master for faults, or on his death to accompany him into the other world ; yet apart from these risks they may ultimately succeed to their owner's property and position. If the owner be their father, he has some care for their future. Under mother-right his own children, by free women, will succeed to the property and position of their mother's brothers. But his slaves and the children of his slaves, will have no such resource. For the latter, therefore, if he have any affection for them, he makes provision in his lifetime, or by the expression of his dying will. Where slavery is general this leads to a custom which, becoming prevalent, may result in changing the line of descent. Where a man dies without children, a trusted and confidential slave whose relations with his owner have been much like those of a favourite child, easily succeeds. Among the Fantis of West Africa, whose descent follows the mother, the chief slave inherits, even where there are children by free women ; for the children belong to their mothers' family and succeed to them and their kin, and not to the fathers.[1]

Under polygyny, in which numerous savage peoples live, the widows who are not put to death (as some at all events of them may be) to accompany their deceased lord, form an important part of the heritage. In such an event they are distributed among the heirs or the next of kin. From this distribution, the sons are by no means excluded, thought a son as a rule does not get his own mother in the quality of wife. If she be aged, she may as his mother enter his household and be supported by him. If she be comparatively young she may become wife to a son by another woman. It is very common that the widows fall to the deceased man's brothers. This custom (called the levirate) is limited by the growth of civilization to cases where the husband has died childless ; and, as among the Hindus and the Israelites, its object is to raise up seed to the deceased, to secure the family property and (at least among the Hindus) to ensure the performance of its correlative duty, the maintenance of the ancestral rites. The eldest son of such a connexion is accordingly regarded as the son of the deceased, and among the later laws of the Hindus the connexion was supposed to cease when its object had been thus attained. There are even, in our eyes, more extraordinary methods for

[1] Post, " Afr. Jurisp.," II, 6, citing Bowdich.

the same object pursued among several Asiatic and African peoples. But the origin of the levirate is wider. It is founded in the help given by the kindred (clan or family) to acquire, by purchase or force, a bride for one of their members. Thus the Bantu of South Africa hold that the most honourable kind of marriage is by payment of a bride-price (called *lobola*). Without this a man has no claim to exclusive possession of his bride, or to the children that may be born of her. The bride-price received by a father for his daughter is not strictly speaking purchase-money. Its payment does not render her a slave. Rather it operates as a guarantee of her good treatment. For, if unable to agree with her husband, she run away, he will lose both her and the bride-price, unless he can satisfy her kin that the fault is upon her, when they will either compel her to return, or restore the bride-price. When the bridegroom pays the bride-price it is divided among the kin of the bride, the principal share going to her father ; daughters are therefore desired as a source of wealth. Much of this wealth, however, is spent in paying the bride-price of wives for sons, or of additional wives for their father. To these bride-prices the members of the kin, who receive shares of the bride-price of daughters, contribute ; and it is a reason frequently alleged in support of the claim to the widows that the claimant, or those from whom he claims, have paid a share of their bride-price. In an early stage of culture, in fact, it would seem that the bride is either purchased or captured by the kin conjointly for one of their number, and that thus they have claims upon her, which arise on the death of her husband, if not sometimes before. But this is a question still under discussion.

Finally, a word may be said on the subject of the transfer of property. An early form of transfer is by means of barter, or the exchange of goods directly, without any medium of exchange or currency. Where commercial transactions become common (and many barbarous peoples speedily acquire commercial habits) some sort of currency is necessary. Various materials have been used for this purpose by more or less civilized peoples. Such articles and materials as cattle, bars of metal, pieces of leather, minted coins, and ultimately paper spring to the mind, and need not be here discussed. Among the less civilized, the objects most widely employed are cowry shells. They are very extensively used in Africa ; and in the French possessions in West Africa, the official rate of exchange for the five-franc piece, in which the native tax is paid, was before the recent great war, 5,000 cowries, though the ordinary rate was as low as 4,000 or even 3,500. In ancient times in Japan *maga-tama*, or curved jewels, of chalcedony, jasper, nephrite, chrysoprase, cornelian, and similar stones seem to have been used ; nor is it quite clear that their use was extinct in the Liu-Kiu Islands prior to the Japanese occupation about twenty years ago.[1] Usually objects used for currency have some intrinsic value, such as mats, sticks of tobacco, and other commercial articles. But there are exceptions to this rule. The only value of cowries, of wampum, dentalium, and other shells used on the American continent, or of mussel-shells used in Melanesia, is that conferred upon them by the labour of gathering and transporting them and, in the case of wampum, of grinding and shaping the beads into which they were

[1] Figured by Aston, " Nihongi," I, 38.

formed. Perhaps the most extraordinary currency is that in use on the Islands of Yap, or Uap, an outlier of the Caroline Archipelago. It consists of disks of limestone or arragonik, quarried in Babelthuap, one of the Pellew Islands, four hundred miles away. These disks vary in size from one foot to twelve feet in diameter, and are each perforated with a central hole, through which a pole is inserted strong enough to facilitate the transportation. This cumbrous money has no value apart from the show of riches it provides, which is rendered the more easy in inverse ratio to the difficulty of stealing it.[1]

[1] W. H. Furness, " Island of Stone Money," 93 ; Christian, " Caroline Islands," 236, 255, 256, 291.

CHAPTER V

INTERNATIONAL RELATIONS

THE attitude of a savage tribe towards aliens, whether as a body or individually, is very simple : it is one of suspicion and hostility. Such is the attitude of the lower animals, due doubtless to the countless dangers of forest and mountain and prairie. In man it may be atavistic, looking back to the æons of pre-human existence, and fortified by all too frequent human experience of treachery and violence. This attitude is reported all over the world. What Dobrizoffer says of the Abipones is, with few exceptions, universally true : " Every stranger whatsoever, Indian, Spaniard, or Portuguese, they suspect of hostile intentions and receive in arms, believing every other race their enemies and designers on their freedom." When the author proposed to take shelter with an old friendly chief : " You would keep away from my dwelling," answered the old man, " if you knew the peril that awaits you there. My countrymen are of an evil disposition ; they want to slay, slay, slay all strangers." [1] Nor is it only that hostile intentions—at least in the sense of physical violence—are feared : all manner of evil magic is suspected. A stranger who

[1] Dobrizoffer, I, 63, 67. Cf. Whiffen, 256, 257.

comes to a community in Morocco is held to be a sorcerer, and is put to death. If he be fortunate enough to escape this fate the hostile natives seek to conciliate him and make use of him as a physician.[1]

A stranger, moreover, as such, is under a taboo and cannot without preparation, or perhaps at all, be admitted into intimacy and still less to take part, even as a silent witness only, in religious rites. For he is endowed with a potentiality, an *orenda* in the Iroquoian phrase, which is unknown, and which may be of evil significance. Among the Bantu of Loango, his dead body will hardly be given burial, because, as Dr. Pechuel-Loesche remarks, admitting the body will be admitting the soul, and who knows what the consequence of that would be?[2] The expulsion of living strangers from solemn rites is a common incident in savage and barbarous tribes. In ancient Rome at certain sacrifices strangers were, with captives and women, required to depart;[3] and in the surviving ritual of the Umbrian city of Iguvium (now Gubbio) the magistrate is directed in the ordinance for the *lustratio populi* to expel all members of certain neighbouring communities by a thrice-repeated proclamation.[4] Such was, and still is in the lower culture, the hatred, distrust and fear of strangers—a feeling by no means absent from the highest civilization, and one which the recent unhappy war has done not a little to intensify.

But this attitude to strangers in general is by no

---

[1] Doutté, 49.   Cf. Weeks, " Congo Cannibals," 176.
[2] Pechuel-Loesche, 210.
[3] Fowler, " Religious Exper." 30.
[4] Bower, 133, quoting the ritual.

means incompatible with kind and generous hospitality to individuals. " Perhaps no people," Morgan says, " ever carried this principle to the same degree of universality as did the Iroquois. Their houses were not only open to each other at all hours of the day and of the night, but also to the wayfarer and the stranger." The first duty on welcoming a guest was to offer him food ; and the hospitality they showed to strangers of their own race they offered equally to the intrusive European without fee or reward. " It made no difference at what hour of the day, or how numerous the calls, this courtesy was extended to every comer, and was the first act of attention bestowed. This custom was universal, in fact one of the laws of their social system ; and a neglect on the part of the wife [for it was she on whom the duty fell] to observe it, was regarded both as a breach of hospitality and as a personal affront. . . . A stranger would be thus entertained without charge as long as he was pleased to remain." [1] The praise that Morgan gives to the Iroquois is equally deserved by peoples in every quarter of the globe, though not by all. The Baganda "welcomed strangers and showed hospitality to guests ; every visitor was given a female goat at least when he arrived—it was not polite to give a male animal—and they never looked for nor expected a return present." [2]

Notwithstanding this, it is necessary usually for the guests ceremonially to purge themselves of the taboo attaching to them as strangers. This is done in a variety of ways. It may be as simple as that of the Somali, who establish a sort of temporary kinship with

[1] Morgan, " League," I, 318, 319.
[2] Roscoe, " Baganda," 6.

a guest by means of the host's spitting in his right hand
and rubbing the saliva on the guest's forehead. Once
thus received into the community, the guest is formally
regarded as a child of the tribe. He is hospitably
entertained ; and when he departs he receives, especially
among the allied tribe of the Oromó, a really valuable
gift.[1]   On the other hand, the rite may be as formidable
as that of the Eskimos, among whom a guest previously
unknown is met by his host, who strikes him a violent
blow on the side of the face. The guest reciprocates
and the contest is continued by alternate blows until
one of the men confesses himself vanquished. The
stranger is then welcomed with a feast.[2] A similar
custom is described in Chukchi tales, and seems to have
been followed among the Chukchi.[3]

It may be added that in a certain stage of culture
there is an alternative possibility to the hostile magical
powers of a stranger. He may be a supernatural being,
in which case his errand is probably a friendly one. He
is then repulsed or ill-treated at the peril of the host, of
which examples are found in the traditions of many
nations. On the contrary, the entertainment of such
a stranger may result in the conferment of great
benefits.[4]

When a stranger has once been accepted as a guest
and his taboo taken off, there arise between him and his
host the rights and duties of mutual loyalty and protection. These rights and duties might be illustrated

---

[1] Paulitschke, I, 246.

[2] Boas, " R. B. E.," VI, 609.

[3] " Jesup Exped.," VII, 582. Cf. van Gennep, " Rites de
Passage," 38–40.

[4] Hartland, " Ritual and Belief," 285 ; " Encyc. Bibl.," IV,
4670 ; Westermarck, " Moral Ideas," I, 583.

from many quarters ; but they stand out prominently in the laws of the Arabs and have been in a measure familiar to every one from childhood in the pages of the Bible and the "Arabian Nights." Penetration into the Arab tent assures to the guest protection against an enemy seeking to wrong him or inflict any harm. Commensality of host and guest is a pledge of fidelity between them, assuring each of them of the just and friendly dealing of the other. The duties and liabilities involved are incumbent upon them both, not merely so long as the guest is within the tent, but afterwards until he has presumably digested the bread and salt of the host, which he has eaten ; and the protection they confer contributes not a little, we are told, to give security to the deserts in which the Arabs wander. Breach of these duties by either party involves a disgrace which cannot be wiped out, if not a crime.[1]

So much for the mutual treatment and responsibilities of individuals. The relations of tribes and peoples to one another are often of the most formal and courteous character, as in civilized diplomacy. In Australia messengers, duly accredited, are sent from one tribe to another for a variety of purposes—to call meetings for deliberation on matters of common interest, to make important announcements, as of a death, to summon assemblies for initiation of the youth, and as ambassadors to settle outstanding questions in dispute. They carry sticks or other emblems of their office ; and their persons are generally sacred. But for better security messengers are preferably chosen who have relatives or friends in the tribe to which they are accredited. With this object also women are often the intermediaries

[1] Janssen, 82–93.

between hostile tribes ; and it is understood that if
they are successful in their mission there will be a time
of licence between them and the men of the tribe to which
they are accredited.[1]

A similar formality and courtesy characterized
the North American tribes, particularly the Iroquois
about whose proceedings we are well informed. Their
famous league consisted of a number of independent
nations whose autonomy was jealously preserved. By
the sachems, or chiefs, and to them, envoys to and from
foreign nations were sent. If it were determined
that the proposition they desired to submit was of
sufficient importance to authorize a council-meeting of
the league, runners, accredited with belts of wampum,
were sent out to the various nations of the league
to summon them to meet on a certain day at a certain
place to consider it. The foreign envoy, or the representative of a nation belonging to the league, who
desired to submit a proposal to the league, would then
be heard with patience and close attention, the question
would be fully debated, and a reply given.[2]

All peoples in the lower culture are not so reasonable.
Many treat foreigners and opponents with disdain and
tolerate no intercourse with them. They hurry to
war on the slightest pretence—often without any sort
of provocation : hostility to strangers is dominant, the
passion for war is supreme. In which case, as we have
found out even among nations pretending to civilization, civility goes by the board ; there is only left the
mailed fist and the rattling sword.

Nor is this overbearing conduct by any means a

[1] Howitt, " S. E. Australia," 678–691.
[2] Morgan, " League," I, 104–106.

special characteristic of the lowest peoples. The Toradjas of Mid-Celebes are by no means on the lowest step of culture, and they are a most quarrelsome people. They are said to live more in war than in peace. They were nominally subject to different neighbouring potentates, yet they troubled little about them beyond paying certain tribute and going to their assistance in war—the latter an obligation they very readily honoured. Subject to this, every village was practically independent ; and if the inhabitants were not exactly at variance with one related tribe, it was easy to find another with which they were in continual hostility. Anything might lead to war. The Toradja is as sensitive about his honour as Sir Lucius O'Trigger. Until the island came effectively under the Dutch Government, in a dispute one word led to another and war was declared before the parties realized their position. Undoubtedly much, though not all, depended on the coolness of the chiefs who were involved. A circumspect and calm chieftain would make all the difference to the issue of a quarrel. Without the soothing influence of such a one there was constant war. Disputes about a debt or a fine, or a refusal of, or delay in, payment, or a quarrel about a wine-palm would be quite sufficient. And where these trivial matters gave occasion to war, graver causes, even deliberate provocations, were not wanting. A man of a friendly community would be slain under the excuse that he was mistaken for an enemy ; or one of two antagonists might compel a neutral to join in and take a side under threat of war, or, in the alternative, if the real enemy were at a distance, might attack an unconcerned and unoffending community near at hand, under pretence that it had given assistance to the real enemy, so that it would be possible to wage war without going far from home.[1] In Australia, war was usually made between tribes or one section of a tribe with another tribe or section of a tribe over their women, or for an alleged murder by witchcraft. Since death was never believed to be from natural causes, however old or infirm a man might be, or from accident, but was always reputed to be by witchcraft of some other tribe, such deaths almost invariably led to attempted revenge and were a most fruitful cause of war. War was never made by the Australian natives for territory or for the subjugation of one tribe by another. In New Zealand, as we have seen, and also in Melanesia, it was made to obtain the bodies of enemies for a cannibal feast, but also to exalt the power and glory of the chiefs who plotted and led the attack against unsuspecting foes. This reason is enough among military peoples in the lower culture, though in Europe it must be disguised under the pretext of defending an aggression from without, or some other equally plausible excuse. The Vikings did not need even this for their raids in the old days : they went frankly and without shame from lust of fighting and the hope of plunder and renown. Among the negroes of West Africa and in Mexico a sufficient excuse was found in the desire to obtain prisioners to sacrifice to the gods. But indeed any excuse, or none at all, is sufficient wherever men desire to fight and are easily organized for that purpose, and where they have nothing more urgent to occupy their energies. Industries, trading, and agriculture throw difficulties in the way of military adventures,

[1] Adriani en Kruyt, I, 201.

though there are seasons in which agricultural communities rest from their labours and have leisure to turn their attention to enterprises against their neighbours.

No general rule can be laid down as to the methods of waging war permissible in these stages of civilization. Treachery and cruelty may be said to be universal. No formal declaration of war is necessary. To fall unexpectedly upon a peaceful village, to pillage, burn, slay, before their victims can recover from their surprise, and to do as much damage, and seize as much plunder, or as many trophies, as possible is the height of heroism. Very often these expeditions are confined to a single raid. Retaliations of the same kind are inevitable, leading to a state of chronic warfare between neighbours. Throughout Indonesia the object of a raid is to procure heads of slaughtered foes, which are then made the objects of religious ceremonies, and the unfortunates thus sacrificed are thought to become benign protectors of their slayers. Among tribes addicted to head-hunting to procure a head, though by treachery and the slaughter of a woman or child, or of an unarmed and infirm old man, is a proof of valour and capacity which must be given by the aspirant to marriage before he can obtain the hand of the lady he desires. In North America, the equivalent trophy is less cumbersome. The scalp only is torn off the fallen foe, with little regard to whether he may be living or dead ; but no sacred rites are paid to it. Prisoners taken are never exchanged : they are tortured to death, or else adopted into the tribe of their captors in the place of a member who has been killed. A chief among the Yao and other tribes of Central Africa " *declares* war by killing or kidnapping some of his enemies. He may either find them on a journey, or send an expedition to their villages. Deeds of this kind proclaim that a messenger sent to the aggressor will be either slain or sent back mutilated, and all friendly intercourse is at an end. War may be declared on a travelling party by simply calling out *ngondo* (war). The natives *conduct* war by making a series of attacks in order to plunder or to destroy by fire and sword."[1] North American wars are waged with great bitterness. Whole tribes have frequently been rooted out or driven away and their land occupied by the conquerors, causing movement and unrest throughout the continent. Of the Coroados, or Caingang, of Brazil we are told that it is very seldom that one tribe lives in peace and friendship with the others, for an unimportant matter is enough to set up conflicts between them. In the past they have waged without compassion wars of annihilation between themselves; this is one of the chief causes of a great diminution of their numbers in this State. Indeed, the Roman Catholic missionaries claim that in recent years a frightful massacre, in consequence of a quarrel about a woman, was only prevented by the presence of a missionary and the respect in which he was held.[2]

But not everywhere, even among the lowest races, is warfare carried out with this savagery. The South Australian aborigines are, we learn, fearless, but neither bloodthirsty nor ferocious. Apart from mere raids in punishment of a real or supposed murder, their wars consisted of regular appointed battles at places and

[1] Duff Macdonald, I, 193.
[2] " Anthropos," IX, 26.

times previously agreed on. They usually took place about daybreak or towards sunset, rarely lasting for more than three or four hours ; and they were nearly always witnessed by the women and children, and sometimes by other natives who were not concerned in the quarrel. Few of those engaged are killed outright, though deaths from wounds are often numerous. The hostile foes stand face to face and provoke one another with noisy demonstrations and threats ; spears are thrown and warded off or avoided. Finally, wounds may be inflicted or somebody may be killed, and the contest ends. " That their fights seldom terminate fatally must be attributed partly to their skill in warding off the spears and partly to the fact that they have no thirst for bloodshed." [1]   In the Moluccas, where a higher degree of civilization has been attained, the testimony is the same. A community which has determined on war formally challenges the enemy. If the challenge be accepted preparations are made to defend the village. If the hostile forces meet they exasperate one another with satirical songs and taunts until one party attacks the other. In fighting, the effort is not merely to slay as many as possible of the enemy, but to take their heads ; and the conquerors return home with their trophies to feast and celebrate the occasion in triumph. Hostilities may last for years. They consist of raids and the capture of heads, enlivened by occasional battles. When a number of persons have been slaughtered, peace is made, often by the efforts of neighbouring districts, to which the proceedings of the foes are probably inconvenient. [2]   On the Island of

[1] " Native Tribes, S. Australia," 245–247.
[2] Riedel, 104, 233, 425, etc.

Wetar, indeed, to meet a stranger or one of a village belonging to a different district was to take his head, especially if he were thieving wax and honey. The head was often scalped and set up on a stake in the bush ; in war-time (but only then) its flesh was eaten and blood drunk.[1] On the whole, however, wars do not seem to be waged with great savagery and bitterness, or to result in much loss of life. From some of the islands head-taking has disappeared for centuries.

The Trobriand Archipelago to the south-east of New Guinea is inhabited by a people of one tribe only, speaking the same language, having the same customs, intermarrying and participating mutually in all festivities and ceremonies. This close connexion, however, does not prevent their indulging in internecine warfare. The various districts into which the archipelago was divided were frequently at war, and of the two most important we are told that their relations were always strained. A row over gardens, pigs, women, a breach of etiquette or suspected sorcery would result in a preliminary fight on the spot, which might be smoothed over, or might lead to a formal outbreak of war. Each side mustered its forces. " Midway between the two capital villages a place was selected and a circular arena cleared, which would be the theatre of fighting. The opponents ranged themselves opposite each other, at a distance of some thirty to fifty metres apart, and throwing their spears. Behind the warriors stood or sat the women, helping the men with water, coco-nuts, sugar-cane, as well as with verbal encouragement. . . . Fighting lasted as long as both parties could resist the onrush of their opponents. When one party had to

[1] Riedel, 445.

flee, the road to its villages was open, and the enemy would rush on, killing men, women, and children indiscriminately, burning the village and destroying the trees. The only remedy for the defeated party was to abandon their villages and to fly for life into another district. As a rule, practically everybody, especially the defenceless ones, would succeed in escaping. Thus, in 1899 about a dozen villages were destroyed, and the vanquished had to remain homeless for a time. The main village, Omarakana, was not rebuilt before a formal atonement ceremony had been held between the victors and the vanquished, the latter having been living in a provisional village some six miles to the south of their own village."

The natives were neither cannibals nor head-hunters, and therefore lacked not only the two inducements to warfare in that quarter of the world, but also two incentives to prosecute it with ferocity and to initiate it with treachery. Yet they were ardent fighters and conducted systematic and relentless wars. War was, however, carried out with "a considerable amount of fairness and loyalty, there being strict rules of conduct which were scrupulously observed." They were evidently innocent of "Kultur." They never practised nocturnal raids on another village, taking it by surprise and ruthlessly murdering all inhabitants in their sleep —a form of warfare very popular among the majority of Papuasian tribes. Nor would they invite a party from another place and murder them treacherously. They never fought without warning, nor would they fight at night ; and though complete victory—death of the enemies and destruction of their village—was the ultimate aim of a war, the mere fact of fighting as a sport, and the glory derived from a display of daring and skill, were an important incitement to warfare." [1]

Such are the methods of making war in the lower culture, more or less brutal according to the greater or less ferocity of their manners and the excitability of their passions. No convention provides for what acts are permissible and what are not. Desultory warfare may go on for years, or it may terminate in a pitched battle after a few days. But sooner or later both sides get weary; and if one does not submit, means are found to accommodate matters between them. Often the lives lost, and the wounds of the survivors are reckoned up, and the side that has escaped more easily agrees to pay for the overplus of the enemy's losses. This is the method recorded to have been taken by the ancient Norse in making peace, after fighting among themselves. [2] Sometimes each party pays for all the lives it had taken. On the Island of Bougainville (Solomon Archipelago) each life is valued at one hundred fathoms of shell-money, these made of a kind of mussel-shell; and in making peace payment is formally tendered for each life taken, together with additional compensation for the plunder taken. A scaffold is erected on the site of the battle. The strings of money are ceremonially hung openly in view of every one and fetched away as accepted first by one party and then by the other. The proceedings are completed by the opponents chewing betel-nut together and a feast of roast pork. [3]

This constitutes a public ceremony of peace and

[1] Malinowsky, " Man," XX, 10, 11.
[2] Morris, " Ere-Dwellers," 130.
[3] Thurnwald, " Zeits. vergl. Rechtsw.," XXIII, 325–326.

reconciliation. Such a ceremony is necessary formally to end a war ; and its publicity and formality fix it in the minds of all. In North America the ceremony usually consisted in the smoking together of the pipe of peace, after which both belligerents resumed friendly relations. So in Central India the conclusion of hostilities between the Kalār, or Kalwār, now an occupational caste, but perhaps originally an offshoot from the Bania or other Vaishya tribes, and the Bhīls, a non-Aryan, probably Kolarian tribe, was marked by the solemn administration of opium by the priests to all present at the ceremony.[1] The Iban of Borneo on a similar occasion sometimes make a large wooden image of the hornbill, a sacred bird, and hang upon it great numbers of cigarettes. These are taken down during the ceremony and smoked by all the men present.[2] An essential of the conclusion of peace by the Bukana in the north of New Guinea is smoking cigarettes and chewing betel together. In the case of serious inter-tribal conflicts, however, both parties eat together, presents are exchanged, and certain members of either side take up their residence in the villages of the other.[3]

Throughout the eastern hemisphere, however, the most widely spread ceremony of peace-making consists of a sacrifice or of a blood-covenant, or often a mixture of both. Typical of the crudest form of sacrifice may be taken that of the Pomo and the Boumali on the middle course of the Sauga River in the French Congo. There, when peace is concluded between two villages

[1] Russell, " Tribes and Castes, Central Prov.," III, 318.
[2] Hose and McDougall, II, 88.
[3] Neuhauss, III, 445, 446.

that have been at war, the inhabitants, men and women, are assembled in a corner of the forest, a big, fat slave is brought, his head is stuck in the ground, his legs upwards, and he is cut in two vertically, one half of the body is given to each village, and each person, man and woman, eats a piece, and drinks palm-wine to the sound of the tom-toms. On less solemn occasions it is sufficient to cut the prepuce of a boy, and to sprinkle the blood flowing from the wound mingled with palm-wine on the two chiefs, who swear to make war no more, nor to capture wives, or steal kids from one another.[1] Several of the tribes in British territory on the other side of the continent, instead of a slave sacrifice a dog, which is cut in two ; representatives of both sides then take hold of the divided halves of the dog and swear peace and friendship over it.[2] The Wachaga on the sides of Mount Kilimandjaro take a rope which is drawn three or seven times by uncircum-cized boys round an assembly of warriors of both sides and the ends are knotted together so as to enclose the warriors. A kid is then brought and made to stand parallel with one side of the rope. The oath is admini-stered to the men inside the circle, and the kid and rope are cut in two at one stroke. The blood is sprinkled over both sides, and the flesh of the kid is consumed by the old men who superintend the rite. It is said that formerly political leagues were sealed with the blood of uncircumcised children. The ceremony is reported in two different forms. In one an innocent boy and girl, supplied by the district begging for peace, were circumambulated three or seven times by the warriors

[1] " R. E. S.," I, 30, 31.
[2] Frazer, " F. L. Old Test," I, 394, 395.

uttering the words of the oath. The children were then cut into halves and buried on the boundary of the two warring districts, the warriors entering into the engagement afterwards walking over the grave and going home. A milder form of the rite, like that of the tribes on the Sauga, only involved the circumcision of the two children and swearing peace over their blood, which was then drunk mixed with beer. The curse denounced on those who violate the pact appears to be the same in all these forms—death like that of the victims without. offspring—a curse to which the Wachaga are very sensitive.[1]

Sir James Frazer has recently collected and expounded a number of cases of such covenants by sacrifice and the taking of an oath between the divided halves of the victim, taking as the text of his exposition the covenant made by Jahwe with Abram. It appears from his inquiries that, as it was among the ancient Hebrews, so still among many modern peoples in the lower culture this is a very solemn form of covenant, and therefore specially suitable for a treaty of peace.[2] It is not necessary here to discuss the variations assumed by it.

Nor need we delay long over the ceremony of blood-brotherhood. It is well known and widely spread. By it the blood of the parties to the rite is mingled and becomes one, so that they regard each other as really akin. Hence we can readily understand why it is specially appropriate in peace-making, though by no means confined to such occasions. Mr. Weeks gives an account of the formalities on the settlement of peace

---

[1] J. Raum, " Arch. Religionsw.," X, 285–290.
[2] Sir James Frazer, *op. cit.*, I, 392 *sqq.*

between Monsembe and some other towns on the Upper Congo with which there had been war. When the parties met, a stick, called *ndeko*, was carefully scraped and the scrapings were mixed with salt. The headman of each side clasped the other's right hand with the *ndeko* between the palms. Incisions were then made in the arms, the mixture of *ndeko*-scrapings and salt was rubbed on the cuts, and each headman sucked the other's cut for a few moments. Each in turn took the *ndeko*-stick and struck the wrists and knees of the other, saying : " If ever I break this covenant, may I be cursed by having my nose rot off ! " Sugar-cane wine was drunk ; and then " a medicine man took a palm-frond, split it, and put one half of the frond across the path leading from Monsembe to the upper towns—the towns of the contracting parties. This was not only a sign that all that palaver was finished, but it was a fetish having power, it was supposed, to punish anyone who broke the treaty. It was firmly believed that the side that renewed that quarrel would get the worst of it by wounds and death.[1] In the Moluccas there are more forms than one of the blood-covenant. On the Island of Wetar a league between two persons, or two districts, is formed in the presence of the chiefs by the persons concerned, drinking together blood from each of their right hands mixed with kalapa water. Thus they become blood-brothers ; and we are significantly told that the people of the negari [districts] that have taken such an oath cannot marry one another.[2] In case of war between two districts on the Island of Makisar, or Keisar, their representatives bring to the dwelling of the rajah of the island a pig and a sheep.

[1] Weeks, " Congo Cannibals," 73.   [2] Riedel, 446, 447.

The rajah cuts the right ears of these victims and drops some of the blood that flows into a kalapa husk containing koli-water. Praying the tutelary spirit (*mahkarom*) to curse those who violate the peace anew, he spits into the fluid in the kalapa husk, and gives it to the chiefs to drink. After they have done so they kiss the right foot, hand, and breast, and the nose of the rajah, and then each other's right hand and nose. Their followers and people of their district do the same and break out into a great weeping, confessing their fault to the rajah and begging for pardon. The scene ends with a feast and the drinking of more koli-water. Here the blood of the covenanters is not exchanged,[1] but they become of one blood by drinking that of the unhappy pig and sheep. Among the Kayan of Borneo the equivalent ceremony is that of invoking a chicken, and with a sword striking off its head, and then smearing the right arms of the men with the bloody blade.[2] To end hostilities when one party is victorious, the Jabim of New Guinea do not deal in blood : the boldest of the conquerors makes a streak with lime such as is used for chewing with betel on the foreheads of the defeated party, lest they should be exposed to the arbitrary action of the spirits, who might affect the growth of their dogs and pigs and loosen their own teeth.[3]

Whether after these elaborate rites, after these oaths and curses, faith was kept by the contracting parties must probably be answered differently in each case. Not all peoples in the lower culture can be accused of breach of faith. The Iroquois are illustrious for their unwavering fidelity to treaties. Both with aboriginal

---

[1] Riedel, 425.   [2] Hose and McDougall, II, 66.
[3] Neuhauss, III, 318.

nations and with the white intruders they frequently entered into treaties. " All of these national compacts," says Morgan, " were ' talked into ' strings of wampum, to use the Indian expression, after which these were delivered into the custody of the Onondaga sachem, who was made hereditary keeper of the wampum at the institution of the league ; and from him and his successors was to be sought their interpretation from generation to generation." North American nations on making a treaty always exchanged belts, which were not only the ratification, but the memorandum of the compact.[1] It was the business of the official keeper of the wampum to remember its exact meaning, and to recall and translate it into speech on all proper occasions.

[1] Morgan, " League," I, 327.

CHAPTER VI

SANCTION

THE famous definition of Law formulated by the great English jurist, John Austin, and ultimately derived from the seventeenth-century philosopher, Hobbes, treats it as a rule prescribed by a sovereign to his subjects, who are necessarily obnoxious to the sanction enforcing the law and the duty of obedience.[1] This definition had in view the conditions of a civilized community, and it was long accepted in British juridical philosophy. But anthropological researches and the relations of the State with a large number of savage and semi-savage peoples have, since Austin's day, widened the scientific outlook and rendered necessary a new definition, in which account has been taken of the conditions of life in relatively primitive communities. In such communities law is not the act of a sovereign, whether an individual or a body of men : it is the traditional rule of the community ; and it is enforced, not by a sanction prescribed *ad hoc* by the sovereign, but one that is involved in the beliefs and practices of the community. Having summarized the laws of such communities, our next business is to consider the sanctions by which they

[1] Austin, " Jurisprudence," I, 316, 317.

are enforced, and which are by no means always the same in kind as those of civilization.

The indistinction already noticed between provinces of primitive law that we should regard as wholly disparate is a characteristic which is at the base of savage thought. The "primitive" mind perceives resemblances more quickly and fully than it perceives differences; it apprehends and accepts wholes which we should analyse into parts in order to understand them; it unites where we should divide. This synthetic attitude renders every part of the civilization of a relatively primitive people indivisible without great difficulty from the rest. It draws no line between law and morality, religion, medicine, or art. All these are part of the social and mental fabric, and the traditions by which they are governed are the same. The savage is far from being the free and unfettered creature of Rousseau's imagination. On the contrary, he is hemmed in on every side by the customs of his people, he is bound in the chains of immemorial tradition, not merely in his social relations, but in his religion, his medicine, his industry, his art: in short, every aspect of his life. These fetters are accepted by him as a matter of course; he never seeks to break forth. To some of them there are definite sanctions, to others none; but he does not distinguish between them. To the civilized man the same observations may very often apply; but the civilized man is too restless, too desirous of change, too eager to question his environment, to remain long in the attitude of acquiescence. By the action of many generations his reverence for the thing that is, and for the wisdom of his ancestors which produced it, has been sensibly reduced; and he has no

mentality is not ours. With him, in the absence of exact knowledge, mysticism holds undisputed sway. The mystical relations of men and things are conceded by all ; and they are the most important, the supreme relations. We must expect to find, therefore, that the " primitive's " view of human conduct differs from ours, that many of his laws are incommensurate with ours, and that they are enforced with sanctions incomprehensible to us. We must not, however, forget that all sanctions, even those that we call supernatural sanctions, are sanctions imposed by society ; and they derive their power from the universal conviction of their reality, a belief so strong as to give them very often an automatic operation.

We may divide the sanctions attaching to laws in the lower culture into several classes. First come evils held to be intrinsically connected with the violation of a law. The Arunta forbid the eating by a man of the flesh of any animal which has been killed or handled, or even seen, by certain relatives ; and as these relatives are reckoned according to the classificatory system, by which relationships are almost universally reckoned in the lower culture, the prohibition is very wide. If he violated it " the food would disagree with him, and he would sicken and suffer severely, a belief which has the result of securing the observance of the custom," the intention of which is to assist in regulating the supply of food.[1] Boys who have been recently initiated are prohibited among many—perhaps all—Australian tribes for a time from eating the flesh of certain animals under similar sanctions. The sanction, however, among

[1] Spencer and Gillen, " Central Tribes," 469.

some tribes, such as a branch of the Kulin, is that the boy infringing the taboo of the spiny ant-eater or the black duck would be killed by thunder, or if of the female opossum, or native bear, he would be liable to fall when climbing trees—sanctions which come within the next category to be considered. The object is to discipline the youths, and to reserve the best food for the old men.[1] Another illustration is afforded by the Jajaurung of Victoria, by whom, "whenever a female child was promised in marriage to any man, from that very hour neither he nor the child's mother [was] permitted to look upon or hear each other speak, nor hear their names mentioned by others ; for if they did, they would immediately grow prematurely old and die."[2] The intention here apparently is to prevent marriage or sexual intercourse between the parties to the taboo. The sanctions in these cases are, so far as appears, automatic in their action. There is no hint of any interference on the part of any supernatural being ; there is certainly no overt interference on the part of society. The prohibition, it is true, is in the social interests ; but the sanction really operates to prevent its violation entirely by the intensity of the belief held and insisted on by society in the threatened consequences. A similar terror is inspired by the *tapu* which hedges the sanctity of a Maori chief. Well authenticated instances are known in which persons unwittingly guilty of violating the *tapu* have died from fright.[3]

[1] Spencer and Gillen, "Central Tribes," 470 ; cf. V. Strehlow, 7 ; Howitt, " S. E. Australia," 612.
[2] Brough Smyth, II, 156 ; Taplin, " N. T. S. Australia," 32–34.
[3] Taylor, " Te-ika-a-Mani," 164.

Another class of cases must not be confounded with the foregoing, though the "primitives" themselves do not always seem clearly to distinguish them. It is that in which the sanction is believed to be enforced by some power we denominate supernatural. Mourning ceremonies all over the lower culture—ceremonies sometimes very uncomfortable and even painful to the survivors—are carried out in fear of vengeance for neglect by the ghost of the deceased. This is explicitly stated in regard to the frenzied lamentations and serious wounds of mourners among the Arunta ; [1] as well as to similar rites in other parts of the world. Reference has just been made to the food-restrictions imposed on youths who have undergone the ceremonies of initiation, the sanctions of which differ in various parts of Australia. The tribes about Maryborough in Queensland prohibit the eating of emus' eggs, and threaten that if the youths even break an emu's egg, "the offended spirits will shortly raise a storm of thunder and lightning, in which the unlucky culprit will probably be struck down." [2] Among the Yuin, "the novices were told that if they [ate] any of the forbidden animals, the *Joia* [magical power] belonging to it would get into them and kill them." [3] The tribes about Maryborough say that a supernatural being called Kohin "is offended by any one taking a wife from the prohibited sub-class, or not wearing the mourning necklace for the prescribed period, or eating forbidden food. Such offences bring on the offender Kohin's anger, and sooner or later the person dies in consequence." [4] The effect of the terror

---

[1] Spencer and Gillen, "Central Tribes," 510.
[2] Howitt, "S. E. Austr.," 606 ; Curr, II, 377.
[3] Howitt, *op. cit.*, 560. [4] *Ibid.*, 498.

was so great that Howitt records that he knew of fatal cases " produced by what one must call conscience in novices who had broken the rules and eaten of forbidden food " ; but he gives no information about the cases or the tribes in which they occurred.[1] Some tribes, however, did not leave the breach to the sanction of supernatural penalties and the operation of conscience ; they definitely threatened death—and they performed it.[2]

The supernatural sanction thus becomes an effective safeguard of social rules, whether it take the form of punishment by mystical impersonal power, or by ghosts or other imaginary beings. It is rooted in the beliefs of the people, it segregates the offender from society by the mysterious horror it creates. In higher civilizations it is attributed to the anger and vengeance of the gods. Tales of their vengeance, sometimes lighter, sometimes heavier, are found all over the world. The lighter kinds of vengeance may be exemplified in the beliefs of the Barée-speaking Toradjas of Celebes, whose chief industry is agriculture, and whose thoughts are said to be all concentrated on their rice-fields. Everything they do for the gods and the spirits of the deceased turns to the benefit of their rice-fields ; on the other hand, every transgression of morals, or of established custom, is visited by the gods on their crops.[3] Various breaches of sexual morality—adultery,

---

[1] Howitt, " S. E. Austr.," 639. He does, however, mention subsequently the case reported to him of a young Kurnai, who had " stolen some female possum which he was not yet permitted to eat and who lay down, and within three weeks literally died of fright " (ibid. 769).

[2] Ibid., 583, 594.

[3] Adriani en Kruyt, II, 229.

incest, and others—are frequently held to be punished
by the gods by rendering the guilty persons barren,
or by the infliction on the whole community of the
more serious penalty of a plague of wild and ferocious
animals, excessive rain or drought involving destruction
to the crops, earthquakes, or epidemics. Such consequences can only be stayed or altogether averted by
special rites of atonement, or by the death of the guilty ;
and they lead thus in many cases to the execution of
the criminals. This appears to have been the belief
of the Hebrews and of the Greeks ; and it is abundantly
exemplified among peoples of the lower culture in
modern times. Nor is the belief in such supernatural
interference confined by any means to sexual trespass.
Other high crimes and misdemeanours, especially when
committed by kings and rulers, bring down the vengeance of the gods in a similar way, as when King David
caused a pestilence by daring to take a census of his
people. The wrongful or even accidental taking of
human life excites the horror of the community. A
murder is deemed to entail pursuit by the ghost of the
victim—a superstition not wholly eradicated from a
high stage of civilization, and one that among various
African tribes compels even warriors returning from a
battle in which they have slain foes to undergo rites of
purification. In British Columbia a Ntlakapamux who
has killed an enemy in battle fears that the vengeance
of the dead man would strike him blind, unless
he propitiated the ghost by painting his face
black. The neighbouring Lillovet entertain the same
belief.[1]

A sanction of a more tangible, though perhaps not

[1] " Jesup Exped.," I, 357 ; II, 235.

more effective, kind is the execution or bodily mutilation of the offender by the direct action of society through its recognized officials. Among "primitives," dwelling for the most part in frail wooden buildings, there are often no means of a milder punishment by incarceration. Hence death or mutilation, or sometimes a severe flogging, is the only corporeal sanction that can be employed to secure the observance of law. Such a sanction is freely employed, and, it need hardly be said, with a brutality at which we shudder, and against crimes we do not recognize as such, or treat very lightly. I do not pause over such offences as that of adultery with the wife of an African ruler : the corresponding crime is recognized by British law as high treason, and is punishable by death, though for other reasons than operate on the negro mind. By the Hebrew laws, any adultery of a married woman entailed the death of both parties. Any departure from established custom, any infringement of the observances held binding upon a member of the community, is viewed as a serious matter, and one that must be punished, if need be, should the threat of mysterious consequences be insufficient to restrain it, by the sharpest reprisals of society. Allusion has already been made to the ritual prohibition of the Australian tribes, generally sufficiently ensured by threats of supernatural consequences, but in case of necessity enforced, by some tribes at least, by death. In fact, ritual prohibitions have, among many nations, if not everywhere, been enforced by corporal punishments. Their object is at all costs to preserve in all its traditional details the national or tribal religion. The gods are jealous and irritable beings, easily offended and hard to be appeased.

It is needless to search for illustrations. The old Hebrew legislation, comparatively humane among semi-civilized peoples, is replete with Draconian prescriptions, of which the penalty of death imposed upon the profaner of the Sabbath is by no means the only, or perhaps the most atrocious, example ; and the Mosaic law in more respects than one has for generations set the tune to which Christian Europe has danced. We need not therefore be surprised if in lowlier societies ritual ordinances are precisely and literally enforced by extreme and relentless penalties.

Nor are these penalties confined to wilful or reckless infringement. " Primitives" draw no strict line of demarcation between voluntary and involuntary offences : a certain degree of civilization is necessary to distinguish between them.[1] Society looks at the thing done, and does not—at least in the lowest stages of evolutionary development—often trouble itself with motives. Accidental homicide is confounded with wilful murder, evokes the same passion, and is followed with the same consequences. What is true of homicide is true of other offences. It is recorded that in the Kingdom of Porto Novo on the Slave Coast of West Africa, early in the eighth decade of the last century, a young man accidentally killed a python. Now a python is worshipped as the manifestation of the god Dañh-gbi, and the priests of the god, in whose hands the vindication of his divine majesty rested, sentenced the culprit to be burned alive. But he escaped and put himself under the king's protection. The king took his part, and succeeded in imposing his will on the priests,

[1] For example, " Zeits. vergl. Rechtsw.," XXXV, 27, citing Dias de Carcalho.

though he earned their permanent ill-will which eventually cost him his life.[1]

The distinction between wilful murder and more or less venial homicide marks an advance in civilization, such as is found in the provisions of the Hebrew law relating to the cities of refuge, provisions which in their form bear witness to the difficulty of imposing upon a barbarous people such an amelioration of the ancient law.[2] Thus among the Nabaloi Igorot of Luzon a wilful murderer was hanged with circumstances of barbarity, but one found guilty only of what we should call justifiable homicide was merely condemned to pay the funeral ceremonies of the man he had killed. If two men fought and they were both at fault, and one was killed, the survivor was hanged ; nor was the fact of both being drunken allowed to excuse the survivor. Yet strangely enough we find it laid down that if a man went to the house of another, and fought with, and killed him, the slayer was not punished, beyond being condemned to pay for the funeral ceremonies. In such a case our law would deem the acts of the slayer evidence of wilful murder, and he would be uncommonly lucky if he escaped.[3] There can hardly be any mistake, for the reporter is no hasty or passing traveller, but an American official who has lived for more than twelve years among the people, and has taken pains to learn their dialects and to study their customs and beliefs. Moreover, he gives the native text of these and other laws. As he does not comment on this law, we must conclude that he does not notice what seems to us

[1] Ellis, " Ewe," 145.
[2] Exod. xxi, 12–14 ; Num. xxxv, 6, 9–34.
[3] " Univ. Cal. Pub.," 257.

the inconsistency, or cannot explain it. Likewise the Elgeyo of East Africa do not allow the family of a murdered man unlimited right of vengeance. The elders fine the murderer thirty-seven goats, which he pays presumably out of his own stock, or by the help of his own family. These are divided among the murdered man's relations, and over and above them if he be the owner of cattle he must give a cow to his victim's mother —a symbol " that she may bear another child to replace the lost one." But this is not sufficient, for in addition the murdered man's family is at liberty to burn his house and to slaughter and devour his live stock. Such vengeance would not be permitted in the case of un-intentional homicide. The elders would impose a fine of a minimum of five goats for the benefit of the deceased's family ; and with that they would apparently have to be satisfied.[1]

Crimes against a god are often only expiable by sacrificing the criminal. Such were not only the killing of a sacred animal, as in the case mentioned above. In ancient Mexico, the theft of gold or jewels was held to be a crime against the god Xipe. The criminal was accordingly made a human sacrifice at the feast which the goldsmiths celebrated in honour of the god in question. He became taboo to the god, and such a death was regarded as honourable.[2]

It is a well-recognized principle in civilized law that ignorance of the law is not allowed to excuse a breach. So essential is this for the due administration of justice and the preservation of peace that it is not surprising

---

[1] " J. Afr. Soc.," **XX,** 198. As to compounding in this way, see *infra*, p. 154, *sqq.*

[2] " Zeits. vergl. Rechtsw.," **XXXVII,** 446, *sqq.*

to find it recognized also in the lower culture.[1]   There
it is often exceedingly troublesome, for the laws and
customs of various peoples are so widely different that
a stranger from another country is not unlikely to find
that actions which are perfectly innocent in his own
land are not permissible—are even highly criminal—
among a tribe whose customs are unknown to him.
Thus it is reckoned by the Ba-ila, a Bantu people in
Central Africa, a serious thing when a hunter has killed
an elephant, to pass at the back of the animal as it lies
dead, or to make remarks about, or laugh at, the appearance of its buttocks.[2]   The offender will be seized and
held to ransom for such an offence.   A similar offence
is committed, not only by stealing, which obviously no
one could deny knowing to be an offence, but by
damaging, even involuntarily, accidentally and un-
consciously, a " medicine " or a receptacle of medicine
belonging to another.   Anyone who knows the strange
and unexpected objects sometimes regarded as " medicine " will appreciate the wide door this opens to what
we should regard, and what many a native belonging to
another tribe would regard, as preposterous claims.[3]
After this it seems a comparatively reasonable claim,
when a visitor at a strange village was charged by a
savage cow and to defend himself snatched up a stool
and struck the beast, but had the ill-luck to break the
stool, that the owner at once seized him and tied him
up, demanding a cow as a ransom for the damage to
an article of comparatively small value.   But, as the
authors to whom we are indebted for the record observe,

[1] For example, " Univ. Cal. Pub.," XV, 239, among the
Nabaloi Igorot of Luzon.
[2] Smith and Dale, I, 395.   [3] *Ibid., loc. cit.*

" we have to remember that what seems trivial to us is in their eyes very precious. And it is not so much the value of the thing that a Mwila looks at, as the fact that it is his, and nobody has the right to interfere with it or damage it. This of course the visitor knew ; he was in fault, though life or limb may have been at stake ; and all he could do was to protest against the exaggerated value put by the man upon his piece of furniture which was damaged in defending himself." [1]

The vindictive feeling of some societies (not always the lowest) is not satisfied with death as a punishment for some offences. It pursues the criminal after death by the denial of funeral rites. The dead man is entitled to proper funeral rites. Among the Dyaks of Borneo they must celebrate these rites, in order that the soul may have rest, and the inhabitants of the spirit world may associate with him.[2] The Tarahumares of Mexico celebrate three functions (a woman requires four) to bid a formal farewell to the dead, and to chase them off to the end of the earth, where the place of the dead is. They are supplied with food and drink for their journey, and are expected to go off to their rest and to leave the survivors in peace. " If the feasts were not given, the departed would continue to wander about in animal shape " ; and a story is told of one unhappy man who had changed into a lion (puma ?).[3] It is therefore as much to the interest of the survivors as of the deceased that the rites be performed. In Northern Nigeria " the spirits of the dead would find no rest unless

---

[1] *Ibid.*, 392, 394.

[2] Grabowsky, " Internat. Arch.," II, 188 ; " Anthropos.," I, 23.

[3] Lumholtz, " Unk. Mexico," I, 383–390.

honoured in the proper fashion . . . and if they are
not treated properly they will certainly vent their
displeasure upon their neglectful relatives." [1] The
Bulgarians believe that the souls of those who have not
been properly buried by the priest remain for ever on
the earth.[2] Similar beliefs are found in the Tyrol,[3]
in France,[4] and indeed all over Europe, no less than
among " primitives." Accordingly a denial of burial
rites is a serious additional punishment, even when a
criminal has been executed by an atrocious death. It
is a punishment for the survivors as well as for the
criminal himself. This barbarism is only practised as
a rule upon the bodies of such whose deeds excite the
special horror of society. A part of the vengeance
upon enemies commonly reported of savage societies
is to stick their heads on poles and leave them there as
a warning to others. The most brutal dismemberment
of criminals and outlaws was usually performed by the
Germans and other tribes who overwhelmed the decaying
Roman Empire.[5] It lasted through and beyond the
Middle Ages in most if not all the states of Europe.
Criminals convicted of various offences, especially
treason, were subjected to this last indignity. In our
own country to be hanged, drawn, and quartered, or to
be hanged in chains until their bodies dropped piecemeal
away was an all too common sentence ; and after the
Jacobite rebellions of the eighteenth century the heads
of executed leaders were to be seen on Temple Bar.

[1] Tremearne, " Tailed Head-hunters," 190.

[2] Strausz, " Bulgaren," 453.

[3] Zingerle, " Sitten," 54.

[4] Laisuelle de la Salle, " Centre de la France," II, 91.

[5] "Zeits. vergl. Rechtsw.," XXXIII, 359-367, where the
matter is fully discussed.

In the burning of heretics, part of the Church's hate found its gratification in the impossibility of gathering and performing burial rites over the ashes of the victims.

As civilization advances, the extreme penalty of death or mutilation is in many cases mitigated or compounded for. The involuntary crime of giving birth to twins, usually held to be evidence of adultery, or frequently a monstrous birth involving a portent of supernatural displeasure only to be mollified by the instant destruction of mother and babes, is compounded for in West Africa by the extinction of one of the children, either the first-born of the two who is looked upon as specifically the adultrine issue, or the weaker of the two (the girl, if the children are of different sex), and, with or without killing either of the children, by the banishment of the offending mother. Banishment, however, whether for this or any other crime, is a penalty hardly less terrible than death. In a society founded on kinship, natural or artificial, as a society in the lower culture is, a person whose ties of kinship are not recognized by his proper community is an outcast and an alien from all. He meets with nothing but universal hostility, and his death is certain, if not by violence, at any rate by slow starvation and misery alone in the forest or the wilderness. Analogous to this fate is that of expulsion from caste in India. The victim suffers, often from what in another social organization would be regarded as a trifling violation of ritual requirements, a universal boycott. No one will consort with him, no one will speak to him, no one will minister to him in his utmost need. His nearest kin repudiate him. They dare not approach him on any pretence, lest they themselves be also put out of caste. For this boycott, as in the case of taboo in other lands, is a most infectious disease, immediately communicated to all who come into contact with him, and to the very vessels and implements which he uses. From its terrible consequences, however, the caste usually provides, except in cases of persistent and impenitent disregard of caste rules, a way of escape, by submission, and the performance of certain rites (including a substantial dinner to the caste-brethren at the offender's expense), after which he is received back into caste and nothing more is said.

In a society where trade and industry have created wealth two more mitigations remain—fine and slavery. Fine as a sanction is an alternative by which wealthy men often escape the death penalty. The ancient English and Welsh laws, like those of most of the nations founded on the ruins of the Roman Empire, contain elaborate scales in which the lives of persons of different ranks of society, from the king downwards, were valued, and other crimes were treated on similar principles. The Wabende, a Bantu tribe on Lake Tanganyika, cultivate the ground, fish the lake and trade, undertaking even short trading journeys. So much are they accustomed to this, that it is somewhat of a disgrace to any man who has never been outside his native village. Murder is in theory liable to be punished by blood vengeance. It is limited in case of murder of an ordinary man to reprisals upon the offender himself, but the murder of a petty king (*moami*) involves the offender's entire family. But the crime is capable of being compounded for on payment of the blood-price. It rests with the chief who has jurisdiction at the place to decide whether the *lex talionis* shall be enforced, or whether a compensation shall be accepted ; and if the injured kin in spite of the chief's decision to the contrary slay the offender it will itself have to pay the blood-price for so doing. For very serious wounds and bodily injuries death is likewise the nominal penalty, but for all other crimes there is a regular tariff. In case of murder if the murderer himself cannot pay the blood-price, his relatives must help him. If they cannot pay between them, the murderer, his wife, and children are enslaved.[1]

It is very often supposed that this method of treating crime, and especially murder, implies merely a carelessness of the value of human life and security. In a state of society in which men always go about with arms, and must be always more or less on the alert against enemies and lawless men, it does imply that men must be content to take the risks of a disturbed condition of the peace, to defend themselves and their property against attack, and not depend entirely upon the impersonal protection of the law. But it means much more. Murder, accidental homicide, violations of property, assaults, wounding—from which an individual suffers—are resented by the whole force of his kin and lead to blood-feuds that convulse the entire community and may culminate in the most disastrous results. As society becomes more and more closely organized, it views with increasing alarm the consequences of these feuds. Measures to terminate them become necessary. As a means to this a price is fixed, a rough valuation is made by which the lives of different ranks and other crimes than homicide are appraised ; and

[1] " Anthropos," I, XI, 98, 106.

the man who is found guilty is condemned to payment. Such a society has not yet emerged from collective responsibility. The criminal is, whether voluntarily or compulsorily, helped to pay by his kin, and the fine goes to the head of the State, if the State as such effectively exists, or is divided among the relatives and dependants of the victim of his crime. A criminal unable himself to pay, and destitute of kin who will, or can, help him, is deprived of liberty and becomes a slave. His position is analogous to that of a defaulting debtor on a civil contract, for in such a society the penalties are founded, as a French writer of authority remarks, " not on the idea of punishment but on that of compensation." [1] The position of a slave varies greatly among different peoples. In West Africa, where slavery was known long before intercourse took place with the peoples of Europe, it was essential to the equilibrium and prosperity of the social system. But it was a very different thing from that which we are wont to imagine it. We may take as typical Baoulé, a part of the French possessions of the Ivory Coast, and inhabited by a branch of the Agui. There the slaves were all aliens purchased from adjacent countries, and therefore not likely to receive as good treatment as if they were fellow-countrymen. Yet we are told that they " are treated with the greatest gentleness, and that especially if they have been bought young and show themselves docile, they resemble much more the old family servants of our romances, who make part of the household, than the word *slave*—that is to say, human cattle—presents to our eyes. As children they share the food and the games of their master's children ; as adolescents

[1] Clozel and Villamur, 435.

they are only compelled to the small labours in which their master's children equally take part ; as adults, if they be women, they help the wives and daughters of their master in the household work or the lesser work of the fields, they may marry their master, and in that event they live on the same footing as the free wives ; if they wed a slave they are usually sent with their husband to a plantation, where they build a hut and dwell with their children, cultivating the soil at once on their master's and their own account, till the hut becomes a hamlet, the original couple grow into a family, and these slaves become in reality farmers. At other times the adult male slave is employed by his master in commerce. If he show himself able in this capacity he soon receives from the master a kind of percentage on the returns of his trade ; he may thus become rich, buy slaves for himself and set up in business on his own account. The slave who is an expert manual labourer is left absolutely free, provided he share his gains with his master. Finally, a born diplomat who aids his master with his counsels, rapidly gains his confidence, and is feared and respected almost equally with his master." In short, " the slave is a client in the Roman sense, a servant without wages, but supported by his master and making part of his family rather than a veritable slave." " A master speaks of his slaves as ' my sons,' or ' my young men,' or ' my men ' ; and they speak of him as ' my father.' To be sure, these slaves have been bought and may be sold again ; but there are no slave-markets such as our imagination shudders at. The children of slaves are, however, inalienable, and their children are free. Among some tribes, where there are no heirs, a slave may succeed to the property of his master. On the other hand, among other tribes, at the master's death, some of his slaves were liable to be slain to accompany him in the grave. If either of these customs ever was practised by the Agui they do not appear now to be part of their jurisprudence.[1] The mild character of slavery about Lunda, lower down on the West Coast, has been recorded by a Portuguese traveller, who says that the impression left is rather that of servants than slaves, for the slaves sit at their master's table with him, wear his clothing, carry his weapons, hunt, and have like him a voice in the decisions of the commonwealth. Here the child of a slave is reckoned, as among the Agui, a child of the master ; and a man who had no other means of livelihood would give himself into slavery. The ceremony for this purpose was simple. He had nothing more to do than to break a cup or bowl belonging to a free man ; he thereupon became his slave, and might be sold as such to a passing caravan of traders.[2]

The slave-trade on the west coast of Africa was not originated by Europeans. It was originated and organized by the natives themselves, and existed before the discovery on and about the Guinea coast. To such an extent did it prevail that not only was the slave-market large, but also slaves were treated as currency for the trade in other objects.[3] Slavery became the ordinary punishment for various crimes, among which adultery is said to have been the principal support of

[1] Clozel and Villamur, 130–132.

[2] " Zeits. vergl. Rechtsw.," XXXV, 4, citing Dias de Carvalho, XXXIV, 469, citing Gamitto, " Diary of Port. Exped. commanded by Major Monteiro."

[3] *Ibid.*, XXXV, 4, XXXI, 355.

it in Fanti-land.[1] Another crime thus commonly
punished was theft.[2] Captives in war had to submit
to the same fate. To Negroes and Bantu alike on the
west coast of Africa it was a recognized practice, if a man
made default in payment of a fine or a judgment-debt,
that one of his kin might be seized and sold into slavery,
redeemable if ever he had the means. He might give
one or more of his children (or where the line of descent
ran through the mother, as it more commonly does, one
of his sister's children) into a kind of qualified slavery
as a pledge for the fulfilment of his obligations, unless
he became, as he frequently did, himself the pawn.
The pawn then worked for certain days as a slave to
the creditor, and the rest on his own account, until he
was able to redeem himself. The law as to the rights of
creditor and debtor and pawn naturally differed among
the various tribes ; but this mode of giving security
is very usual, and men who have lost all by gambling
(a popular vice in the lower culture) often adopt it.[3]
Some of these tribes, however, are sufficiently advanced
to deposit goods in pledge for debts, or even to have an
equivalent to our practice of levying an execution on
the debtor's goods to enforce' a judgment.

Slavery, as has often been pointed out, could not have
been literally a primitive custom. It is founded in a
distinction of classes, implies the accumulation of wealth
and in general, though not invariably, is dependent on a
settled rather than a nomadic condition. It has,
however, been a widespread institution, persisting into

[1] *Ibid.*, XXXI, 360.
[2] *Ibid*, XXXIV, 279, 458.
[3] *Ibid.*, XXXV, 4 ; Ellis, " Eẅe," 218–222 ; Clozel and
Villamur, 129, 130, 160, 180, 221–222, 295, 321, 338, 339, 336,
415–417, 469–471, 518 ; Sarbah, 95, 96.

a high state of civilization, even to our own day. Africa, to its misfortune, has been its home and hearth ; but in many other places it has been deeply rooted. Probably it began in an amelioration of the practices of war : a defeated foe ceased to be massacred when it was found to be more advantageous to give him his life and employ him as a slave. Out of this would grow the custom of making raids for the purchase of capturing slaves. This is well established in the west of Africa. It existed among the north-western tribes of North America, and for many ages among various European peoples. In north-western America there was a regular traffic in slaves ; but the slaves were usually well treated ; they might even purchase their freedom if they could raise the means ; sometimes rich men would free their slaves. On the other hand, a slave had no rights (he seldom has, especially in the lower culture) and might consequently be maimed or killed by his master without the latter being called to account by anyone. Among the Tlingit, as among the Maori of New Zealand, it was quite a common thing for a chief to kill slaves and bury them beneath the supporting posts of his house in the course of its erection. Some tribes at least on a chief's death, killed and buried with him his favourite slaves, as in other parts of the world.[1]

In mediaeval Europe slavery was largely practised : in England it existed almost to the Reformation—at least in the form of serfdom. Serfs were *adscripti glebæ*. They could not be sold apart from the land on which they dwelt and worked, and in which they had

---

[1] These rules are usefully summarized in the " Handbook of American Indians, North of Mexico," " Bull. B. E.," 30, II, 597–600 (art. " Slavery," by H. W. Henshaw).

rights gradually won from the law—rights which descended in the modified form of copyhold tenure to the present day. Personal slavery, to be sure, was gradually limited and finally extinguished much sooner. The laws of Anglo-Saxon kings early frowned on the stealing of men ; and Cnut, if the code of Winchester attributed to him may be trusted, definitely forbade the selling of Christian men into exile or to heathen.[1] The Church, though it never set itself against slavery as such, made a virtue of the freeing of slaves ; and from time to time rich slave-owners on their death-beds, when they themselves had no further use for them, freed their slaves with the approval of the Church. It failed, however, to set the example.

There is yet another sanction in the quiver of the law, not a supernatural or corporeal sanction, nor one which involves the forfeiture of goods or of freedom, but a very real and serious sanction nevertheless, namely ridicule and contempt. In a small and intimate society ridicule is a very potent weapon ; and the savage in many such societies is extremely sensitive to it. The contempt of the community is hard enough to bear in a society like our own where the victim may perhaps escape to a different society which does not know his previous history and does not therefore share the feeling with which he is regarded at home, and where in any case there are a thousand other interests to dislocate and interrupt the attention of his fellows. It is insupportable in a society where every one knows every one else, and where, beyond the provision for the day's needs, all thoughts and all conversation are fixed upon one's immediate companions and one's relations with them,

[1] Schmid, " Gesetze an Angelsachsen," 273.

and whence there is no escape. In such a society ridicule and contempt are an effective punishment, from which every one would be most desirous to be free. We are told of the Eskimo of Greenland that " no court of justice was established as a special authority to secure the maintenance of the laws. With the exception of the part which the *angakoks*, or the relatives of an offended person, took in inflicting punishment upon the delinquent, public opinion formed the judgment-seat, the general punishment consisting in the offenders being shamed in the eye of the people." [1] The chief means by which they were brought to book consisted of satirical songs, frequently called from the ancient practice of the Scandinavian peoples, *nith-songs*. These songs were sung, among others, on festival occasions. They were used " for settling all kinds of quarrels and punishing any sort of crime or breach of public order or custom, with the exception of those which could only be expiated by death in shape of the blood-revenge. If a person had a complaint against another, he forth-with composed a song about it and invited his opponent to meet him, announcing the time and place where he would sing against him. Generally, and always in cases of importance, both sides had their assistants, who, having prepared themselves for this task, could act their parts if their principals happened to be exhausted. These songs also were accompanied by drum-playing and dancing. The cheering or dissent of the assembly at once represented the judgment as well as the punishment." [2] " In these songs," says Dr. Nansen, " which as a rule were composed before-

[1] Rink, " Tales and Trad.," 32, 33.
[2] *Ibid.*, 34.

hand, but were sometimes improvised, they related all the misdeeds of their opponent and tried in every possible way to make him ridiculous. The one who got the audience to laugh most at his jibes or invectives was the conqueror. Even such serious crimes as murder were often expiated in this way. It may appear to us a somewhat mild form of punishment ; but for this people, with their marked sense of honour, it was sufficient ; for the worst thing that can happen to a Greenlander is to be made ridiculous in the eyes of his fellows, and to be scoffed at by them. It has even happened that a man has been forced to go into exile by reason of a defeat in a drum-dance. This drum-dance is still to be found upon the east coast. It seems clear that it must be an exceedingly desirable institution ; and for my part I only wish that it could be introduced into Europe ; for a quicker and easier fashion of settling quarrels, and punishing evil-doers it is difficult to imagine." [1]

At the opposite end of the habitable globe the Australian Blackfellow is equally sensitive to the ridicule and contempt of his fellows ; and this sensitiveness is amply used to enforce the law. The excessive mourning ceremonies, so characteristic of savages, are specially remarkable among them. Prostrations, wailing, wounds, severe cuts on their heads with fighting clubs, painting with pipeclay are usual methods of expressing the grief of mourners among the Arunta. They are certainly enforced by the fear of the ghost. But another and very potent sanction is the attitude of society to anyone who dares to omit these and the accompanying ceremonies. We are told that there is

[1] Nansen, " Eskimo Life," 187.

nothing to which a Blackfellow is so sensitive as to the
contempt and ridicule to which non-compliance with a
custom such as this will expose him. But it must not
be forgotten that he also fears " that unless a sufficient
amount of grief be displayed he will be harmed by the
offended spirit of the dead man." [1]

The power of ridicule and contempt as a sanction for
the compliance with tribal law is exemplified abundantly
in savage society. While it is unnecessary to give
further illustrations of it, it is perhaps not unnecessary
to remark that ridicule and contempt may be very often
the essential punishment in many cases where to us
the penalty seems of obviously another kind. Thus,
the Dacota of North America prohibit the address of
certain relatives by name ; and the punishment for
infringement is stated to have been that the offender
had all his (or her) clothes cut off his (or her) back and
thrown away. [2] Here it seems clear that much more
serious than the loss of the clothes would be the indignity
and the ridicule of society.

Some peoples attach great importance to the confession of any transgression of the law. Among the
Eskimo of Baffin Land and Hudson Bay a breach of
custom can even be atoned for by public confession.
According to Dr. Boas, this has arisen from the infectious
character of a breach of taboo. To prevent the consequences of mingling with others after breaking a taboo,
such as coming into contact with a dead body, or
bleeding, or (if a woman) menstruating, or the consequences of some minor infringement of tribal morality,

[1] Spencer and Gillen, " Central Tribes," 510.
[2] Frazer, " Totemism and Exogamy," III, quoting a contribution to Schoolcraft's " Indian Tribes."

public announcement of the fact was required to be made ; and this " has gradually led to the idea that a transgression, or we might say a sin, can be atoned for by confession. This is one of the most remarkable traits among the religious beliefs of the Central Eskimo. There are innumerable tales of starvation brought about by the transgression of a taboo. In vain the hunters try to supply their family with food ; gales and drifting snow make their endeavours fruitless. Finally, the help of the *angakok* [shaman or priest] is invoked, and he discovers that the cause of the misfortune of the people is due to the transgression of a taboo. Then the guilty one is searched for. If he confess, all is well : the weather moderates, and the seals allow themselves to be caught ; but if he obstinately maintains his innocence, his death alone will soothe the wrath of the offended deity."[1] Certain tribes of Togo on the Slave Coast of West Africa hold that marriage within the same totem-clan is incest ; and it is strictly forbidden. As such sexual offences are often believed to do, it causes a drought. When this occurs, the guilty woman is led first to the market and then to some of the temples of the gods, and there made to confess her crime aloud, weeping.[2]

Dangers and crises in the individual life, as distinguished from the life of the community, are frequently only to be got over by confession of trespasses committed, it may be, years before. Thus it is a common rule among the Negroes and Bantu that a woman at confinement is required to confess any adultery that she may at any time have committed,

---

[1] Boas, " Bull. Am. Mus. Nat. Hist.," XV, 120, 121.
[2] " Anthropos," VI, 456.

especially if there be any difficulty or delay in the birth. If she deny any adultery, we are explicitly told by the Anganja about Lake Nyasa and the Thonga of Southeast Africa that she may die ; if she own up and give the name of the man her fault will be at an end : the child will be born. Sometimes the husband likewise is made to confess, lest his wife die.[1]

In these and other cases the mere act of confession is held to relieve the wrong-doer, if not of his sin, at least of the consequences of his guilt. A similar idea, that of obtaining good luck, followed a curious custom of the North American tribe of Crows. The night before sighting the enemy's camp the braves on the warpath were wont to confess the names of the women with whom they had had sexual relations. The other men present, among whom might be the husbands of the faithless women, were sworn never to reveal the warpath secret to any woman, on pain of death. The oath is said to be strictly observed ; but the husband, if inclined to give trouble, might leave an erring wife.[2]

---

[1] " J. R. A. I.," XL, 306 ; "Man," XII, 150 ; Junod, "R. E. S.," I, 150.
[3] Lowie, " Anthrop. Pap. Am. Mus. N. H.," IX, 224. The Blackfeet have a similar custom. *Ibid.*, VII, 65, 289.

CHAPTER VII

PROCEDURE

THE administration of law in every organized community demands a regular and orderly procedure, both for civil and criminal purposes. A society destitute of such a procedure to enforce compliance with its rules or to punish non-compliance is in a state of chaos : it will be a prey to individual caprice and brute power. The consent and authority of the collectivity behind the law are necessary ; and they can only be given, or at all events evidenced, by the punctual observance of the proper forms. This is so well understood in all civilized countries that a special branch of the law has been elaborated, called *adjective* or *auxiliary law*, dealing with the kinds of procedure and the forms and methods to be employed in the administration of the *substantive law*. It is not to be expected that the administration of the law in savage and barbarous societies shall be surrounded with all the safeguards and formalities with which we are familiar. Crude and rough as they may be—as, indeed, they necessarily are, particularly in the lowest stages of culture—they are nevertheless the forms recognized for procuring the punishment of infractions of the tribal law, or for obtaining reparation of wrong.

Everybody in the society knows what these forms are, and how they may be invoked.

In the early stages there is no distinction between civil and criminal procedure. When as yet no wealth has been accumulated, when property in land, as distinguished from the right of occupation by the tribe or its sections, is unknown, when a man's possessions are merely the rude tools and ornaments which he has in constant use, the subjects of dispute are confined to women, to personal affronts, or to violence, or else to breach of tribal taboos affecting the life of the tribe or of some section of it. The public is directly affected; its internal peace is imperilled; and the complaints which come before the representatives of the community are in the nature of criminal complaints. As civilization advances, the forms devised for the ruder stages are gradually adapted to deal with matters previously unknown and undistinguished. Procedure for one purpose is applied to another, because no clear distinction has yet been perceived between crime and personal questions of right and wrong only affecting very indirectly the well-being of the community. Default in payment of a debt is visited with a penalty as great as robbery or adultery; and murder is measured by rules of compensation, as if it were not different in kind, but only in degree, from a breach of contract or simple trespass.

Another difference between our law—indeed, the law of all civilized countries—and the law of primitive peoples, which may be briefly noticed here, is that the latter have no Statute of Limitations. When once a claim of right has arisen it may lie dormant for any length of time, it may be pursued after any interval, until it has been finally decided. The " primitive " recognizes no justice in barring his claim by mere lapse of time or dilatoriness in prosecuting his suit. He considers that the prosecution of his suit should be left to his own convenience. Time is not so filled for him with interests and with labours as it is with us, nor does he admit the public advantage of fixing a limit within which his claim must be brought forward and pressed to a decision, so as to produce confidence in daily life and the regular intercourse and transactions of his fellows. Even in the comparatively advanced civilization of Passununah and Rejang, two contiguous districts of Sumatra, where the most respectable form of marriage depends upon the payment by the bride-groom of a bride-price, or *jujur*, to the family of the bride, long credit is, as we have seen, frequently given. " Sometimes it remains unadjusted to the second and third generation ; and it is not uncommon to see a man suing for the *jujur* of the sister of his grandfather. These debts constitute, in fact, the chief part of their substance ; and a person is esteemed rich who has several of them due to him for his daughters, sisters, aunts, and great-aunts." [1] Among the Nabaloi of Luzon, it is not unknown to claim payment of debts alleged to be due to the claimant's great-great-grandfather. [2] The principle of limitation of actions in order to obtain an end of litigation does not appeal to peoples who are, as many " primitives " are, fond of litigation. It is quite modern in jurisprudence. It has not existed in our own legislation for much more than two centuries and a half ; and among the more ignorant of our own

---

[1] Marsden, " Sumatra," 259.
[2] " Univ. Cal. Pub.," XV, 257 n.

fellow-countrymen it has not yet become popular. Any practitioner of the law can recall cases within his own knowledge where it has been defied—not of course, with success, though greatly to the annoyance and inconvenience of the legitimate holders of property whom the claimants worried with their attentions.

The Eskimo are doubtless the least quarrelsome people on earth. It is only human, however, to disagree ; and even they have their disagreements. We saw in the last chapter how they decided quarrels and punished the disagreeable members of an Eskimo community. That highly original method not merely provided a sanction for their laws, but it is itself, we are told, a "primitive judicial process," the popular verdict of which carries a severe and sufficient penalty.[1] If a man cannot be reached by it, if his conduct be such as to render him generally obnoxious, there is a more drastic way of dealing with him, and one that is resorted to with persons accused of witchcraft (black magic). To put any man to death in the ordinary way is a breach of order that arouses a blood-feud. But against a person of this character who has become unbearable, a consultation of the community is held behind his back, he is solemnly condemned to die, and executioners are told off to put in force the decision arrived at. It is true the council takes place in his absence and may, if he have friends who do not agree, lead to a blood-feud. It is not usually a serious risk. For in most cases a man fears to make himself disliked, he is conscious of the growing alienation of his place-fellows, and he amends his ways or goes to another settlement before things are driven too far. If not, his conduct

[1] Nansen, "Eskimo Life," 186, 187.

is recognized even by his friends as insufferable, the proceeding is held to be regular and the sentence just ; he is "disposed of by common consent." Inconvenient angákut (wizards) are sometimes dealt with in this manner.[1]

Equally summary is the procedure sometimes adopted by the Australian Blackfellows of the south-western districts of Victoria against a person whose bad conduct has made him a constant anxiety and trouble to the tribe. A consultation is held, and he is put to death.[2] This seems, however, not to be a common occurrence. "Persons accused of wrong-doing get one month's notice to appear before the assembled tribes and be tried, on pain of being outlawed and killed. When a man has been charged with an offence, he goes to the meeting armed with two war-spears, a flat light shield, and a boomerang. If he is found guilty of a private wrong he is painted white," and is required to stand the attacks of the accuser and his friends first delivered in a body simultaneously with spears and boomerangs, and if he succeed in warding them off with his arms (for he appears not to be allowed to hit back) a shield is handed to him, and his opponents then attack him successively with one blow each. "As blood must be spilt to satisfy the injured party, the trial ends on his being hit. After the wound has been dressed, all shake hands and are good friends."[3] The neighbouring tribe of the Narrin-yeri is administered by a *tendi* for every "clan." The

[1] "Bull. Am. Mus. N. H.," XV, 117, 467 ; Cranz, I, 194 ; Rink, 35. But cf. Stefansson, "My Life with the Eskimo," 365.

[2] Dawson, 76.

[3] *Ibid*, 76.

term " clan " is probably used for a local subdivision of the tribe. The *tendi* is the judgment-council of the elders, who are chosen by the " clan." It is presided over by the *rupulle*, or chief, chosen by the *tendi* from among its own members. " All offenders are brought to this tribunal for trial. In case of the slaying by a person or persons of one clan of the member of another clan in time of peace, the fellow-clansmen of the mur-dered man will send to the friends of the murderer and invite them to bring him to trial before the united *tendies*. If, after full inquiry, he is found to have committed the crime, he will be punished according to the degree of guilt. If it were a case of murder with malice aforethought he would be handed over to his own clan, to be put to death by spearing. If it should be what we call manslaughter, he would receive a good thrashing, or be banished from his clan, or be compelled to go to his mother's relations. All cases of infraction of law or custom were tried thus. A common sentence for any public offence was so many blows on the head. A man was compelled to hold his head down to receive the stroke of the waddy, and would be felled like a bullock, then get up and take another and another, until it was a wonder how it was that his skull was not fractured." [1]

Of the Iroquois of North America we are told : " Crimes and offences were so infrequent under their social system, that the Iroquois can scarcely be said to have had a criminal code. Yet there were certain misdemeanours which fell under the judicial cog-nizance of the sachems (chiefs), and were punished by

[1] Taplin, " N. T. S. Australia," 34 ; cf. Howitt, " N. T. S.-E. Australia," 341.

them in proportion to their magnitude. Witchcraft was punishable with death. Any person could take the life of a witch when discovered in the act. If this was not done, a council was called and the witch arraigned before it, in the presence of the accuser. A full confession, with promise of amendment, secured a discharge. But if the accusation was denied, witnesses were called and examined concerning the circumstances of the case ; and if they established the charge, which they rarely failed to do, condemnation followed, with a sentence of death. After the decision of the council the relatives of the witch gave him up to his doom without a murmur. Adultery was punished by whipping ; but the punishment was inflicted upon the woman alone, who was supposed to be the only offender. A council passed upon the question ; and if the charge was sustained, they ordered her to be publicly whipped by persons appointed for the purpose." [1]

After discussing the procedure in cases of murder, which did not materially differ from that of most uncivilized peoples to be referred to further on, Lewis H. Morgan, the eminent American anthropologist whom I am quoting, goes on : " Theft, the most despicable of human crimes, was scarcely known among them. . . . No locks, or bolts, or private repositories were ever necessary for the protection of property among themselves. The lash of public indignation, the severest punishment known to the red man, was the only penalty attached to this dereliction from the path of integrity." [2] There hardly seems to have been any civil procedure

[1] Morgan, " League," I, 321.
[2] *Ibid.*, 324.

as distinguished from the procedure just outlined ; probably there were in fact few individual quarrels serious enough to come before a tribunal. Quarrels between houses or clans would come before the council, like charges of witchcraft or adultery.

Among the Toradjas of Mid-Celebes, a people less primitive, and certainly more litigious than the Iroquois, a different procedure is adopted. Fully weaponed, but with precautions for the maintenance of peace, the plaintiff and defendant, as they may be called, first seek an opportunity of meeting on neutral ground and talking the matter over, through the medium of two young men belonging to neither party but skilled in argument and repartee. This sometimes results in agreement and termination of the dispute.[1] If not, as is more usually the case, a step farther is taken. Recourse is made to an oath. An oath is, not only in Celebes but elsewhere, an appeal to the higher powers for the truth of what the swearer says, and a curse invoked upon himself if it be not the truth or if he fail to perform what he promises by it. It is thus expressed by the Toradja : " Hear, ye gods who are above and who are beneath ! If it be not true what I now say I shall eat no rice or maize this year, I shall be crushed by a falling tree, I shall be eaten by crocodiles, I shall be ruined, or slain by men." When the defendant has taken such an oath as this the accuser who is not quite sure of his case is silent ; an oath to the contrary is not taken. Instead, if he be sure, he presses for an ordeal, or demands a more stringent oath to be taken, to this effect : " O gods above and beneath, if I be in the wrong or speak untruth, may I within

[1] Adriani en Kruyt, I, 170.

one month [or some other period] fall suddenly sick, or let some misfortune happen to me!" This fixes a definite term for the punishment. If that term run out before the mischief called down from the gods has overtaken the swearer, it is a clear proof that his opponent has laid a false charge against him.[1]

The ordeal has been abolished by the Dutch Government, which is now supreme in Celebes. But formerly it was an alternative to the peremptory oath just described. By the issue of the ordeal the gods themselves were held to show on which side the right was; and it was decisive The ordeals were three in number. The first was only applied to persons accused of witchcraft, among whom were reckoned those accused of being werwolves. A quantity of resin was melted in a pot until it boiled. The accused was brought, an offering of sirih-pinang was made and the gods were invoked to manifest his guilt or innocence. His right hand, except the middle finger, having been enveloped in leaves, the middle finger was put into the boiling resin for an instant. The resin that adhered to it was allowed to grow cold and harden. When it was removed if the finger did not appear burnt it was a certain proof that the accused was no werwolf or witch : otherwise his guilt was clear, he was taken to a lonely spot and hacked to death. The executioners were always men of another tribe, who took away the skull ; for all these peoples were head-hunters.[2] A second ordeal was that of spears. It consisted in a contest between the two parties, which was performed in various ways. The most ancient took place on a piece of ground carefully cleaned of grass. The two parties being set on opposite

[1] *Ibid.*, I, 173.   [2] *Ibid.*, I, 175, 259.

sides the issue was declared, and the gods invoked to
show the truth. The champions being provided with
a number of light spears or laths of komboeno-palm,
first one side and then the other thrust their weapons
into the ground. When all had finished the side which
was found to have thrust its spears most deeply into the
earth won its cause.[1] A third ordeal, less used than
that of the spears, was that of diving. A piece of water
was chosen, not infested with crocodiles, and two
stakes were driven into the bottom. The contesting
parties, or their two champions, dived to these stakes
and took hold of them. He who could remain under
water the longer was successful. The chief of the
village is generally called in by one side or the other ;
he endeavours to settle the dispute by agreement ; in
default he presides at the ordeal. A false accusation
entails a fine.[2]

Among the Negroes and Bantu of Africa the public
trial of disputes and accusations of crime has been
carried to a point more nearly approaching the practice
of civilized nations than that of any other people in the
lower culture. The negro has a keen sense of justice,
a passion for oratory, the gift of eloquence, and the
power of shrewd cross-examination ; and the natives
enjoy the dramatic exhibition involved in a " palaver."
What a British official says of the courts of the Mendi
of West Africa (continued under the British protectorate) is true in general terms of those both of Negroes
and Bantu throughout the continent. " The Mendi
court, when presided over by conscientious judges, has
not only immense power in the country, but is capable
of unravelling matters and arriving at the real facts of

[1] *Ibid.*, I, 175.   [2] *Ibid.*, I, 177.

a case, where the white man might utterly fail. In spite of their primitive simplicity the natives have the means not only of almost compelling witnesses to speak the truth, but of arriving at a more or less correct conclusion as to who is prevaricating and who is committing perjury." And of the native judges of these courts he says : " It is surprising to see with what patience the judges listen to all the facts, how thoroughly matters are thrashed out, and how ingenious the people often are in their prosecution and defence." [1] It may be thought that in these special instances the virtues and success of the native courts are due to the knowledge that the eye of the British Government is upon them, and that an appeal will lie in suitable cases to a British tribunal. But we may be sure that all these characteristics have been built up through many generations of native practice during the long period when they were guided only by their own moral sense, their own institutions, and knowledge that the critical eyes of their fellow-countrymen were upon them.

The same observations apply to the Bantu as to the Negro proper ; the courts are similarly constituted, and though there are variations between them and between the procedure of different tribes, these are comparatively small, and one description will suffice. As elsewhere, there is little or no difference between civil and criminal procedure, except when witchcraft is charged. Witchcraft is a crime which calls forth the strongest feeling of terror and passion ; and the accused is sometimes put to torture and always to the ordeal,

[1] C. B. Wallis, " J. Afr. Soc.," IV, 403, 401. Cf. Smith and Dale, I, 351–355.

usually with fatal results."[1] " I will not pretend,"
says Mr. Junod, " that the Thonga [a Bantu tribe
of the south-east] exactly know the difference between
civil and criminal cases, the same tribunal judging
them both, and all being called by the same name—
milandju. If any distinction is made, it would be
between private and official cases : *private cases* being
those which are settled by the two parties concerned
alone, without the intervention of the chief ; whilst
official cases are those in which the matter has been
brought to the capital."[2] In the year 1880 the Government of Cape Colony appointed a strong commission
to inquire among other things into the native laws and
customs which obtained in the territory annexed to the
Colony. The commission took a large quantity of
evidence and finally reported in the year 1883. Most
of the witnesses spoke in evident admiration of the procedure, one of them saying : " The law-suits are conducted quite as decorously as any I have seen in our
courts. Disturbances are not tolerated."[3] In one
respect it departs, however, from British law—resembling therein the German law, as one of the witnesses,
himself a German, points out—in that every accused in
a criminal case is regarded as guilty until he has proved
his innocence. But it is fair to say that full latitude,
except in cases of witchcraft, is allowed the accused
to do this.[4]

The case is commenced by a formal complaint by an

[1] Post, " Afr. Jurispr.," II, 98.
[2] Junod, " S. A. Tribe," I, 412 ; Cf. " Nat. Laws Com.,"
App. C, 182, 183, 196, 205, 206.
[3] " Nat. Laws Com.," Evid., 158.
[4] *Ibid.*, App. B, 18 ; App. C, 144 ; Smith and Dale, I,
354.

aggrieved person to the chief or his council, whereupon a day is fixed for the hearing and a messenger is dispatched with the insignia of authority and a summons to the defendant and the witnesses to appear on the appointed day. The court is held at the kraal of the chief or an under-chief in the public courtyard, or on the open space in front. The chief or under-chief and his councillors sit in a semicircle,[1] the parties and their advocates and friends opposite one another a little distance away. The witnesses, including the complainant and defendant, or accuser and accused, having been solemnly warned to speak the truth, tell their stories one after another in order and are subjected to severe cross-examination by the members of the tribunal ; all arguments are listened to when offered by the advocates and friends of the parties, often at a wearisome length. When they are finished the chief and his council retire to consider their judgment. Each councillor gives his opinion ; and the chief, who does not always utter his own, but contents himself with taking the advice of his council, delivers the verdict of the court and the judgment upon the accused. Often however the result of the trial is that the defendant or the accused has nothing more to say. That he is in the wrong is so patent that he can only confess and throw himself on the mercy of the court ; or the plaintiff or accuser may find himself in the equivalent position. There is generally an appeal from an under-chief and his council to his superior chief. The fines or moneys

[1] Among some tribes, as the Gaika in the extreme south, criminal cases are tried by the chief alone, in which he is judge, accuser, and prosecutor in one. But such a practice is a rare exception. " Nat. Laws Com.," App. C, 144.

adjudged are levied by the chief, or paid to him. He distributes them to the members of the court, retaining, of course, the lion's share, and pays the plaintiff the amount due to him, first deducting his own share. Thus the costs of the palaver are provided for.[1]

This may be described as the general procedure of Negroes and Bantu, in what we should call both civil and criminal cases.

Of the variations to which I have referred I may mention three. Among the Ba-ila of Central Africa, a Bantu tribe, there is a class of cases that evoke much resentment. These cases do not infringe any taboo strictly so called, but they are personal wrongs which appear thought to involve insults, though directed not always against the person of the wronged, but against his property, or even it may be unintentional. They are called *buditazhi*, a word derived from a verb meaning to enslave oneself. Such a wrong places the person who commits it in the power of the person wronged, and to escape he must redeem himself or be redeemed by his clan. Accordingly the first step in the legal process is to seize the offender or a member of his household, or of his clan, as a slave and hold him to redemption. Negotiations ensue with the view of reducing the claim by the person originally wronged—a claim frequently, if not usually, extortionate and liable to be complicated and aggravated by subsequent events and lawless proceedings on both sides. Ultimately, if the negotiations fail, the matter has to be settled by a judicial " palaver ";

[1] " Nat. Laws Com.," *passim* ; Junod, " S. A. Tribe," I, 410 ; " J. Afr. Soc.," I, 278 ; *ibid*, X, 440 ; " Zeits. vergl. Rechtsw.," XXXI, 356.

or the person seized remains a slave and may form an item in a long list of wrongs involving a number of innocent as well as guilty parties in a fine juridical tangle, passing the wit of anybody to unravel but the most astute native chief reared in the eager and stimulating atmosphere of such disputes.[1]

Among the southern Kikuyu, a Bantu tribe on the slopes of Mount Kenya in British East Africa, the plaintiff, as he may be called, entertains two elders with *njohi*, a drink made from sugar-cane, and commissions them to collect his debt from the debtor. If when they visit the latter he agree to pay, they bring back the stock claimed to the plaintiff's village and there enjoy a further supply of *njohi*. If on the other hand he repudiate the claim or refuse to pay, two other elders are sent to summon the defendant, his witnesses and assessors, and to bring the sheep necessary for court-fees, each party having to pay to the elders fees from one ram upwards to four sheep, according to the amount of the debt or claim. The court consists of a council of three or four elders or assessors chosen by the plaintiff and an equal number chosen by the defendant, apparently without a president. It sits in public on an open grass-plot near the village ; and the onus of proof lies on the plaintiff. Having heard and closely examined both parties and their witnesses, its members retire to an adjacent spot in the bush to discuss their decision, and incidentally kill, cook, and devour the court-fees. When this is done, and a decision has been arrived at, they return to the place where they had been sitting and deliver judgment before the parties and their friends and spectators, announcing the day when two

[1] Smith and Dale, I, 346, 392–395, 401–405.

of the elders will go to enforce it. If the unsuccessful
litigant hand over the sheep or stock awarded, these
two elders will return with two elders of the other
village to consume a goat paid by the successful party ;
and the affair is ended. If, however, the beaten
litigant refuse to obey the order of the court, the elders
who formed it come and with pieces of a certain plant
sweep a public path in sight of the debtor's hut, saying :
" May they (i.e. the goats or stock decreed) be stolen ! "
The following night the successful party is at liberty
to steal if he can the property he claims and congratu-
late the elders on the success of their ceremony. The
ultimate appeal, before the British occupation, was
to arms when the matter could not otherwise be
settled.

On the west side of the continent the cannibal Fang
or Fans, a Bantu tribe that has for many years been
pressing down to the coast between the Ogowe River
and the Cameroons, have a remarkable way of com-
mencing a " palaver." Miss Kingsley, who describes
herself in this connexion as " a wandering student of
early law," gives in her amusing way an example of
its application. She says : " Passing down a branch
of the Karkola River in the Oroungou country in a
canoe with a choice band of natives for crew, we suddenly came upon a gentleman on the bank who equally
suddenly gave several dismal howls, and fired at us with
the scatter-gun prevalent in West Africa." At once
the authoress boldly jumped on the bank, and on the
man fleeing, pursued and caught him before he could
reload. " We found the poor man was merely suffering
under domestic affliction. One of his wives had run
away with a gentleman from a neighbouring village,

and so he had been driven to fire at and attempt to kill
a member of any canoe-crew from yet another village
that might pass his way ; because, according to the
custom of the country, the men of this village would
thereby have to join him in attacking the village of
the man who had stolen his wife."[1] An example given
by another writer presents a more complete idea of
this curious juridical process. " A Fang of the Esisis
clan steals goods or a woman from a Fang of the Nge
clan. The Nge who has been wronged does not go to
the offender for settlement ; he goes to another near
town and shoots the first goat he sees in the street, or
if very angry he may shoot a woman. The owner of
the goat or woman demands of the Nge his reason for
doing so. The Nge replies : ' An Esisis (giving the
man's name) has wronged me ; I put the palaver
(his offence) on you.' The third party then goes to
the Esisis and says : ' An Nge (giving the man's name)
has shot my goat (or woman) because you have made
trouble with him ; he has put your palaver (trouble) on
me. You must pay me ! ' The original offender is
now responsible and liable to two parties. If he is
reasonable they all meet and talk the palaver. If the
palaver is serious, such party appoints his *ntôl* (ambassadors). The palaver is usually talked in the main
street of the town, before all the representatives of
the interested clans, and before all strangers in town.
The Fang are born orators, and remarkable gestures
and orations are made while talking the palaver. The
speaker usually walks backwards and forwards, grasping
and leaning upon a ' palaver-stick.' . . . Sometimes
the *ntôls* (ambassadors) sit in a canoe in the middle of

[1] Introduction to R. E. Dennett's " F. L. of the Fjort," III, iv.

a river or stream and talk the palaver, the injured parties [rather, the parties to the quarrel] being on either side of the stream. The case is talked, the goods demanded in payment stated, and an effort made to *kik nsang* (cut or end the palaver). If they succeed, then the palaver is cut (ended), and a dance follows ; if no agreement is come to, the meeting breaks up and a tribal war exists between these clans." [1]

From this description several things appear. The Fans, a pugnacious tribe, have no judges and no strictly judicial process ; the *ntôls*, or ambassadors, are intermediaries appointed *ad hoc* for the purpose of trying to reconcile the parties, to induce them to agree upon a proper expiation of the wrong, and so of avoiding the else inevitable result of the quarrel—a war between the clans involved. For here, as elsewhere, the clans act with solidarity. It is with intent to involve a third clan, and so to present an overmastering force that the injured party brings another into the dispute : the original wrong-doer then finds himself confronted not only with the party he has wronged, but with a third ; and he knows that, if in the ensuing palaver he fail to satisfy them both, he runs the certain risk of open war by two clans with public opinion behind them against his own clan. He has therefore a very strong motive for coming to terms ; and it usually prevails. The procedure, though not judicial, is conducted in accordance with legal and well-understood forms ; it is regular and effective for the purpose of peaceably settling domestic disputes which would

[1] " J. A. I.," XXIX, 78, 79. A similar proceeding on the Gold Coast, " Zeits. vergl. Rechtsw.," XXXI, 364, citing J. A. de Marrée, " Reizen op de Goudkust," II, 255.

otherwise develop hostilities liable to shatter the whole tribe.[1]

Another method of recovering the payment of a debt or claim—a method which cannot be described as a judicial proceeding, but yet is recognized as according to law and perfectly regular—is practised by the Fanti of the Gold Coast. It consists in the creditor or claimant going early in the morning to his debtor's residence, or the place where he usually follows his occupation. Covered with white clay, or in sackcloth and ashes, he seats himself on a mat, or on the bare ground, with a supply of food enough for a single meal. " He informs the debtor that unless the debt is paid to the last farthing he will not go away ; and if the debtor goes out this creditor follows him everywhere. Instances are known where, the debt not having been paid, the creditor has died of starvation. Sometimes, as the day draws to a close, the creditor swears to commit suicide if the debt be not paid before sunset. If in such a case the debt be not paid, and the creditor doth commit suicide, the debtor is bound to bear the funeral expenses, in addition to paying the original debt and making substantial compensation to the family of the deceased creditor. But when the creditor swears that, if by a certain time the debt be not paid, he and the debtor must both forfeit their lives, the debtor cannot save his life by simply paying the debt, and a compensation : he too must take away his life." [2]

A like proceeding is ancient and well known in Hindu

---

[1] Compare the proceeding among the Melanesians of New Britain for involving a chief in the quarrel and so compelling his interference, Brown, " Mel. and Pol.," 253, 298, 300.

[2] Sarbah, " Fanti Cust. Laws," 94, 95.

law. It is not, to be sure, mentioned by Manu the reputed author of the oldest Hindu code, but it may be referred to under the cryptic expression of " the customary proceeding." [1] It is, however, mentioned, though without details by his early follower Brihaspati, who says : " When (a debtor) has acknowledged a debt, it may be recovered from him by the expedients of friendly expostulation and the rest, by moral suasion, by artful management and by confinement at his house." And he immediately goes on to explain : " When a debtor is caused to pay by the advice of friends or kinsmen, by friendly remonstrances, by constant following, or by (the creditor) starving himself to death, it is termed moral suasion." [2] In India this proceeding of *sitting Dharma*, as it was called, probably owed its origin to the Brahmans, in whose hands it would be a most potent weapon to bring to book a recalcitrant debtor. For the person of a Brahman was sacred, and to cause his death would be to draw down upon the debtor's head spiritual penalties of an awful kind.

An analogous step was also known to the Brehon law of ancient Ireland. A common mode of recovery of a debt in Ireland was by distress. But before distraining, the creditor was obliged to issue an order upon his debtor to pay. Irish etiquette, however, forbade the issue of an order upon persons who were regarded as *nemed*, sacred. In this category were included not only kings and nobles, but also learned men, clergy, story-tellers, poets, lawyers, warriors of the higher grades, and even expert smiths or carpenters ; for these craftsmen were looked upon with awe for their

[1] Manu, VIII, 49 ; " Sac. Bks.," XXV, 202.
[2] Brihaspati, XI, 54, 55 ; " Sac. Bks.," XXXIII, 329, 330.

skill. Accordingly, instead of addressing an order to a debtor belonging to these classes, the creditor went himself and fasted before his door until he paid or gave security for the debt. It was the debtor's duty to offer his creditor food. If he did not pay or give security, the debt was doubled, additional cattle were due for interest, and beyond that he was struck with a sort of curse. On the other hand, if the creditor refused suitable offers by his debtor and still fasted, he lost his debt.[1] The practice of fasting on a debtor, barbarous as we may well think it, was recognized by law and was the product of civilizations that cannot without the misuse of words be properly described as "primitive," though still in a comparatively undeveloped social condition.

It does not seem that evidence is, either among the Bantu or the West African Negroes, ordinarily given on oath. Nor does any disgrace attach to false evidence, though sometimes it may be punished by the chief with a fine or a beating. It is regarded, we are told, very much as we should regard the clever but misleading speech of an advocate. Such a witness is doing his best for his friend.[2] Oaths are, however, taken by the litigants themselves when the case is too knotty for the court to unravel, as well as by others in extra-judicial ceremonies and proceedings. An oath is of the nature of an ordeal. A curse is invoked by the litigant, who swears if he be in the wrong, or by the accused if he be guilty. If he escape the doom thus

---

[1] D'Arbois de Jubainville, " Droit Celtique," I, 264, 268–270, 369, 370 ; *ibid.*, II, 46–48, 220, 281–285.
[2] " Nat. Laws Com.," App. C, 197, 236. But cf. *ibid.*, Evid., 158, 159.

conditionally invoked he is held, as among the Toradjas and many other peoples, to be in the right—he has won his litigation, he is innocent.   When the Gikuyu Council of Elders order the litigants to take an oath because they cannot settle the case, refusal of it by either party decides the dispute against him.   Some of the African oaths involve elaborate and complicated ceremonies. A form given by Mr. Tate, a District Commissioner among the Gikuyu, as applicable to a claim of goats, provides that the parties sit on the ground opposite to one another with their legs intercrossed.   In a hollow made in each of two portions of a banana-skin laid between them the blood of a goat is put, while portions of the flesh and entrails, cut into bits, are kept ready at hand.   An Elder takes a little of the meat and dipping it into the blood touches the defendant with it, and gives it to the plaintiff, who eats it saying : " Goats mine, you are with them ; may I be eaten by this oath, you not being with them ! "   The defendant in his turn, eating a similar portion given him by the Elder replies : " I have not your goats ; may I be eaten by this oath if I am with them ! "   The operation is repeated, plaintiff retorting : " Because you have my goats, if you reach three seasons without having died, may I be eaten by this oath ! " and the defendant returning : " If I die in three seasons you shall be repaid your goats by my children."   If then the defendant die within three seasons he is held to have owed him the goats ; and his heir pays the debt.   Otherwise the claim fails.[1] It is apparent that the oath is regarded as a species of ordeal involving the death by supernatural power of the party swearing falsely.

[1] " Journ. Afr. Soc.," IX, 250.

On the other side of the continent among the Negroes of Calabar, a *ju-ju*, or magical drink called *mbiam*, is administered. The mbiam is not poisonous, but the oath which accompanies it is the most dreaded, and consequently the most respected, of all oaths. Miss Kingsley gives at length its terms as applied to an accusation of witchcraft causing sickness. Before swallowing the drink, which is made of " filth and blood," the accused pronounces a formula denying in precise terms the guilt of causing the illness, or seeking or employing another to cause hurt to the sick man, or making charms, or doing any act of witchcraft, or thinking of it, and winding up with the curse if he have been guilty of any of these things : " Then, Mbiam, *Thou* deal with me ! " She explains that the formula is modified to suit other accusations, but in any case is similarly precise and exhaustive in its expressions.[1]

What we generally know as the ordeal is the ceremonial taking of a poison, or the doing of some act calculated to cause permanent or deadly injury, which is believed only to have effect in case the person who submits to the ordeal is guilty. It is preceded by a solemn inprecation pronounced on himself by the accused, and is made use of all over Africa in deciding various difficult juridical questions—in accusations of witchcraft invariably. The most familiar ordeal is that of poison made from a plant, different among different tribes according to climate and environment, and is so firmly believed in by the natives that they take it willingly, and whole villages have been known to sub-

---

[1] Kingsley, " Travels," 464, 465.   Cf. an analogous ceremony at Accra, on the Gold Coast.   " Zeits. vergl. Rechtsw.," XXXI, 357, 358.

mit to it in a vague charge of witchcraft—perhaps no more than what we should regard as spiteful vitupera- tion. The whole atmosphere is in fact thick with the terror of witchcraft, and every native is eager to rid himself of the suspicion, notwithstanding he knows that in nine cases out of ten the ordeal is a sentence of death. The overwhelming preponderance of fatalities only confirms him to his obsession by the proof it seems to provide of the public danger from the un- suspected number of persons who are guilty of such malpractices. Other ordeals are also used in various accusations as a last resource to determine the question of innocence or guilt. The ordeals of hot iron and boiling water were well known to the Europe of past generations. A form of the latter ordeal is thus de- scribed by Mr. T. J. Alldridge, District Commissioner on the West Coast, as practised in the district of Sherbro, in the Crown Colony of Sierra Leone : " A three-legged iron cauldron is filled with palm-oil and boiled on the fire. Three small iron rings are put into it, a concoction of herbs and leaves is made up and placed in a basin beside it. This concoction is oily. The medicine man takes some of the mixture and rubs it over the right hand of the person who is about to go through the ordeal, who then has to thrust it into the boiling oil and remove one of the rings. If he be successful he is then requested to put it into his mouth ; and if it does not burn his mouth, he is declared to be innocent. If unable to do this without getting burnt he is pronounced guilty, and he is then taken to the *barri* where the native court determines his punishment." [1]

---

[1] Alldridge, 161. For another form of the hot-water test and one of the poison test, see Smith and Dale, I, 356, 357.

The ordeal has been used all over the world. It was recognized in early Hindu law, and various kinds were prescribed according to the caste of the accused. That of boiling oil was similar to the one just described. It was used in Madura as late as in 1813. Another ordeal —that of weighing—is still resorted to in Malabar as a mode of deciding cases connected with caste. Elsewhere in India sundry ordeals are still made use of for juridical and other purposes.[1] In Europe the ordeal was familiar until the end of the Middle Ages—and later in witchcraft cases. The person—most frequently a woman—accused of being a witch was tested by being thrown, bound hand and foot, into a pool of water. Witches were supposed to have renounced their baptism. In that case it was believed that the element of water would not receive them into its bosom. They floated, and were therefore condemned. If, however, they sank they were innocent, but were drowned. The ordeal of water was therefore a most ingeniously contrived and satisfactory means, if not of determining the question of guilt, at all events of getting rid of the accused. It need hardly be said that the ordeal in this as in other matters had the full sanction of the Church. The wager of battle, a judicial duel, was looked upon as a direct appeal to the judgment of heaven. It practically disappeared everywhere at the close of the Middle Ages, but it was suddenly claimed in England in the year 1818 by a man who was accused of murder ; and as it had never been formally abolished he succeeded. Thereupon an Act of Parliament was passed to put an end to it.[2]

[1] Crooke, " Things Indian," 355.
[2] A detailed discussion of the ordeal and its various forms will be found in the series of articles on the subject in the " Encyclopædia of Religion and Ethics," IX, 507 *sqq*.

The solidarity of the kin and the principle of collective responsibility have been already discussed. That collective responsibility should be found all over Africa is what might be expected. The chief wealth of many of the Bantu peoples consists in cattle ; and cattle are naturally the object of raids and the subject of frequent thefts. In such a case it is the owner's endeavour to follow their spoor, or footmarks, and so to trace their destination. The law recognizes this custom and gives effect to the evidence thus obtained. Indeed, the British in South Africa have extended its application in order to protect the property of colonists. The native law requires the owners of the stolen property to follow the spoor whithersoever it goes. When it approaches within a short distance of a kraal they inform the people of the kraal, who are bound to assist in passing it on beyond their kraal to about the same distance. If they refuse to assist, and the owners cannot succeed in tracing it any farther, the people of the kraal are collectively considered as guilty of the robbery, and the charge is at once laid against them. It is not necessary to identify the thief himself, nor even that he should be known. It is sufficient if a prima facie case has been clearly established against a kraal. Indeed, if the thief himself is discovered, and found guilty by judicial proceedings, the fine imposed on him is made up by his kin.[1]

Precisely the same rule of tracing the guilt of the stealing of cattle was applied a thousand years ago in England by our Anglo-Saxon forefathers. The laws of King Athelstan lay it down that if a man who has

[1] Maclean, 63. " Cape Nat. Laws Com.," App. C., 184, 203 f. ; cf. the old Slav law, "Zeits. vergl. Rechtsw.," XXXIII, 299, 300.

lost cattle trace their spoor, or footmarks, into the land of another, the owner of the land must trace it beyond his land if he can ; if he cannot, the spoor is to be conclusive evidence against him. Here, however, there is no question of collective responsibility ; Anglo-Saxon civilization had outgrown that ; but the owner of the land was made liable for the misdemeanours of his dependants.[1]

In the most archaic stage of culture the best guarantee of the maintenance of the peace is afforded by the solidarity of the kin. For, since an offence by or against one member of the kin is looked upon as by or against all, the whole kin on each side is involved, kin is ranged against kin, and a state of warfare is instituted which even the most barbarous and pugnacious of savage may not regard unmoved, and in which a kin that is not very powerful may find itself at the mercy of an angry and relentless foe. The strongest motives are therefore offered to avoid all cause of offence. Moreover, when such a blood-feud has begun, it may end in one or the other kin being wiped out, and in any case it must result in a serious weakening of the community, which will therefore become the less able to make head against its alien foes. The mischief is early perceived, and efforts are frequently made to induce both sides to reconciliation. In this we may perhaps recognize the first step towards the substitution of law for conflict and revenge. The reconciliation thus effected informally by the efforts of influential individuals or the intervention of the tribe becomes more and more the affair of the community. In general assembly or through its chiefs and elders the community gradually

[1] Schmid, 155.

gains arbitral, and ultimately judicial, authority. All sorts of complaints and charges gravitate more and more to the tribunal thus established. Serious offences are treated less and less as grounds of quarrel between kindreds (families or clans), and more and more as crimes against the entire community. The blood-feud gives way to the general sense of the society; and the kin is compelled to postpone its revenge and submit its claims to the authority, whether that authority be embodied in a general assembly, or in a court of the chief only, or of the chief with the assistance of his councillors. This surrender of the right to vengeance is a triumph for law and an upward step towards civilization. At first yielded only by moral compulsion, it ultimately becomes part of the legal system.

The process, however, is slow; and, inasmuch as it is dependent on the circumstances of the people in which it appears, and as the circumstances of no two peoples are exactly alike, and the external influences to which they are subjected differ from tribe to tribe and from community to community, it is irregular, and the degree of civilization and the manner in which it permeates the life of the community vary from one to another. We must never make the mistake of deeming the evolution of civilization as a single and uninterrupted march. The exact course taken by the civilization of any people is the result of its circumstances, of the influences brought to bear upon it, and of the subjects to which from age to age its attention is directed, as well as of its original proclivities. Thus the Ifugao of Luzon—a Malayan people which penetrated the Philippines many centuries ago, and now dwell, on the whole

a peaceable folk, on the sides and in the valleys of steep
mountain-ranges which they have delved and terraced
out with consummate art and infinite patience for the
cultivation of rice and other vegetables, for they are
above all an agricultural people—have never been
driven by stress of war, or the pressure of adjacent
populations, to a high state of organization. In fact,
the only effective institution among them is the kin.
There is no tribunal representing the entire community,
consequently society cannot punish injuries to itself, save
in so far as the censure of public opinion is a punishment. In kinship, however, they have taken several
steps in advance of " primitive " culture. They have
abandoned the clan, if they ever possessed it, for the
clan is unknown to Ifugao law : the organization is
by families, as already described (p. 21 *sqq.*) ; and descent
is now reckoned to include both parents among their
ancestors. The Ifugao claim that much of their customary law and procedure was given them by Lidum,
their great teacher, a deity of the sky-world and an
uncle of their hero-ancestor, Balitok. Unfortunately
the authority to which we are indebted for a knowledge
of Ifugao law omits to delineate the procedure. We
can only conjecture that it began by a consultation of
the members of the aggrieved family, in which the
amount to be demanded of the other side was agreed
upon, and it was followed by a formal demand upon the
offending family. In such a demand success was obtained
by bluff, by cajolery, or by negotiation, or else the claim
was finally repudiated. But repudiation if persisted
in would lead, unless the claim were abandoned, to
open war between the families, and probably a series
of head-hunting raids, resulting in a blood-feud, unless

the intervention of other families, or of influential but unauthorized and unofficial individuals, dreading the consequences of a blood-feud, led to a reopening of negotiations and the ultimate conclusion of peace. But it would seem that the constitution of the Ifugao family claiming both lines of descent must tend to make responsibility more individual than where the family descends wholly from one stock. For in carrying out the principle that the family unity must at all hazards be preserved, regard must be had to the personal position of different members of a family. In a family thus constituted members may belong also more or less nearly to the other family at strife. This will be a very important consideration affecting the enthusiasm with which such a member will enter into the quarrel. Allowance will have to be made for his nearness or remoteness of blood to the relative primarily concerned, the loyalty of the latter to the family group and his consequent popularity in it, and the responsibility or advantage of each member measured according to his nearness in blood to, or remoteness from, the actual aggressor, or other relative primarily concerned —matters generally of small importance in a dispute between two clearly defined groups. The collective responsibility of the family extends the liability to punishment to other individuals than the person chiefly concerned, but Ifugao law is careful to distinguish who are, and who are not, liable to the punishment as a part of the collectivity. It is preferred to let its weight fall on the actual aggressor. But this is not necessary, though it is definitely laid down that only those that are of the nearest degree of kinship may be held responsible. Thus cousins may not be legally punished if there be brothers and sisters of the actual aggressor. With regard to the payment of damages, it is said that "no Ifugao would dream of taking payment for the deliberate or intentional murder of a kinsman. He would be universally condemned if he did so. He would usually accept a payment for an accidental taking of life. There is still however an element of doubt as to whether even in such a case payment would be accepted. For nearly all other offences payments are accepted." [1]

It must be clear that if the Ifugao have not devised a legal machinery for the administration of justice, at least they have risen in many respects to a comparatively high degree of civilized feeling in their attitude towards offences and offenders.

But, returning to the general course of the evolution sketched above, inasmuch as there is yet no distinction between civil and criminal procedure, and punishment is measured in terms of compensation to the party injured, the complainant in a case of murder or manslaughter is the whole kin of the deceased. Compensation must be obtained by reducing the kin of the slayer by the same number by which the kin of the slain has been reduced, or a payment must be made to the latter in currency or other goods. Compensation by payment for a death thus becomes common in all barbarous jurisprudence. It is embodied in all the codes of the kingdoms which were founded on the ruins of the Roman empire. The amount of the wergild, as it was called in England, depended upon the rank of the deceased. The principle extended to injuries and even insults; and elaborate tables are found in the laws,

[1] Barton, " Univ. Cal. Pub.," XV, 14-16.

prescribing these payments. The duty to pursue the slayer involved the right to receive a share of the blood-money ; and this again was co-extensive with the liability to contribute to the blood-money adjudged payable by a member of the kin, in accordance with the principle of the solidarity of the kin. Thus very early in the Middle Ages the blood-feud had begun to be softened by means of the wergild, or blood-money. But the Slav peoples long held out against so unworthy a compromise. To this day the Slavs of Dalmatia and Albania repudiate it, and stand for nothing less than a life for a life, to be obtained by means of, the blood-feud, the more ancient method of revenge.[1] Other barbarians pursue the murderer before the proper tribunal and accept compensation in accordance with its award. The litigious character indeed and forensic abilities of the Negro have popularized the native tribunal everywhere, to such an extent that the blood-feud recedes more and more into the background. Among the Bushongo, a Bantu people of the Congo basin, a few years since, a very able explorer was unable to find a trace of the custom of blood-revenge. Legal proceedings are taken against the person accused of murder. He is tried, and if found guilty may be sentenced to death. In that case he is allowed to be lynched by the crowd outside the royal enclosure, unless he be respited by the king. Drunkenness or insanity, or infancy of the criminal are enough to draw upon him the royal clemency. But the sentence is not necessarily one of death : it may be only a heavy fine payable to the king. Among the Eastern Bushongo

[1] Hartland, " Perseus," II, 426 ; Miss Durham, " J. R. A. I.," XL, 465.

the punishment is hanging, and the executioner is the heir of the victim of the crime ; but the kin may accept a money compensation instead of pressing for the murderer's death. Homicide not amounting to murder is atoned for by a fine ; and in any case drunkenness is considered a mitigating circumstance, and the capital penalty is not inflicted.[1] So far beyond the inexorable Jugo-Slavs have these poor pagan Bantu advanced in civilization.

[1] Torday and Joyce, " Bushongo," 76.

CHAPTER VIII

LEGISLATION

THE peoples whom we call "primitive," as being nearest the presumed original condition of humanity, are proverbially intensely conservative. Ample evidence of this is furnished equally by reports of travellers, missionaries, and scientific inquirers of the present day, and by comparison of their statements with those of the travellers of past generations, back to the sixteenth and seventeenth centuries. Bosman, Brue, Barbot, and Merolla who travelled in West Africa in the seventeenth century, or the early years of the eighteenth, have left us accounts of the customs and conditions of society there which remain accurate with very little modification to-day. The only changes which have been effected have been caused by the advent of Europeans, and their introduction of an alien religion, of tobacco, and of additional food-supplies in the shape of bananas, manioc, and maize. The alien religion has made but very little way. The permanent change it has effected in the native ideas and practice is only to be learned by a minute examination ; on the surface it has produced none at all. Bishop Codrington, comparing the statements of Mendana, the Spaniard who discovered the

Melanesian islands in the latter part of the sixteenth century, with the customs and conditions of society that he himself found four hundred years later in the Solomon Islands, decides that they were essentially unchanged, except that open cannibalism had ceased to be practised in the islands of Florida and Ysabel, and that on most of the islands bows and arrows had given way to spears as weapons of offence.[1]

What is true of these two widely sundered populations is true of others in a similar condition of savagery or lower barbarism. From generation to generation they follow the customs of the fathers. As a recent scientific explorer says of the Tinguians, a pagan tribe of Luzon in the Philippines : " The fact that the ancestors did so-and-so, is sufficient justification for performing any act for which they have no definite explanation." [2] In a corner of southern Mexico are found communities of different tribes in close contact. Aztecs, Otornis, Tepehuas, and Totonacs dwell in adjacent towns, each community with its own language, customs, and costume ; and there are in fact single villages with two, three, or even four different tribes living side by side, and each preserving its own customs, language, beliefs, and even dress.[3] If we are tempted to ascribe this to tribal jealousy or hatred, we have only to turn to comparatively isolated peoples like the Seri of the Californian gulf, or to wholly isolated ones like the Polar Eskimo, to find the same phenomenon. The latter people in particular do not hunt the reindeer, though their neighbourhood teems with the animals,

[1] Codrington, 9.
[2] Fay-Cooper Cole, " Pub. Field Mus. Nat. Hist.," XIV, 26.
[3] F. Starr, " Proc. Davenport Acad.," VIII, 79.

nor fish for salmon which abounds in one lake at least, and which their conquerors under similar conditions make an important part of their food-supply. Their fathers neither hunted reindeer nor fished for salmon —possibly they had abandoned these practices ages before in other circumstances—nor do they ; but they observe taboos and practise complicated customs and ceremonies because their fathers did, and not because there is any utility or reason in the observance or the practice.[1] It would seem as though habit alone were not sufficient to account for this persistence. The inhabitants of the Moluccas in a less secluded situation,[2] and the Bechuana of South Africa [3] in spite of the pressure of the white man for generations, adhere to their ancient customs and regard any departure from them as an insult to their forefathers, whom, in common with many other peoples in the like stages of culture, they worship. But whatever the cause—and other causes may easily be suggested and are known to operate elsewhere—this attachment to old custom is almost universal ; and it is not the less but the more so, as a general rule, the deeper we probe down in savagery.

On the other hand this adherence to the customs and laws of their forefathers is by no means absolute. Its appearance is deceptive to the people themselves. Circumstances are always, if slowly, changing, often so slowly that the people themselves are unaware of the change ; and the laws and customs necessarily change with the circumstances. When this is the case the old superseded practices are forgotten, and the fact

[1] Steensby, 373.   [2] Riedel, 97.
[3] Philip, " Researches," II, 118.

of the change, to say nothing of its details and direction, passes beyond recall. The people believe that they are still following the precepts and example of their most remote ancestors, when the truth is that they have long since abandoned them. At all events it is clear that no people, however backward, is still in a primeval condition. Even the slowest and most conservative of savages have obeyed the law of change which rules the entire human race in a movement on the whole forward, though not without temporary and local relapses due to special conditions, geographical, climatic, or occasioned by the contact and collision of alien communities.

We are here only concerned with this secular process as it has involved changes in the laws of peoples in the lower culture. These laws are unwritten. They depend for their validity on general acceptance and recognition. Formal changes are seldom made. There is no authority universally acknowledged which has power to enact fresh laws over the heads of the community, or against its consent. The customs of the fathers, coming down from an unknown antiquity, enlist on their side every force of conservatism ; and in that stage of civilization the forces of conservatism, strong in every stage, are of overwhelming strength, As we have just seen, in communities where the worship of the dead is part of the vital institutions, as it is in so many cases, the very idea of change in the customs of the fathers and the laws they have handed down is regarded with horror as dishonour, if not treachery, to the gods. Among the Bantu Bangala of the Congo basin, the still more horrifying charge of witchcraft and its inevitable punishment hang over the heads of any who deviate in the smallest measure from the customs and institutions of the tribe.[1] And in Australia, where the natives are far less obsessed by the terror of witchcraft than the African Negroes and Bantu, and where ancestor-worship strictly so called does not exist, they are equally bound hand and foot by custom. What the father did, they must do. Any infringement of custom within certain limitations is visited with sure, and often severe, punishment." [2]

Yet the forces of evolution are, after all, too strong for the most tenacious primitive conservatism. Changes are introduced and accepted by the people. These changes must have been initiated by individuals. A collectivity is but an organized aggregate of individuals ; and the collective opinion and the collective will are formed by the union and concurrence of individual opinions, and individual wills. Sir Baldwin Spencer and Mr. F. J. Gillen, whose emphatic statement of the conservatism of the Australian Blackfellows has just been quoted, go on to say that it is, notwithstanding, possible for changes to be introduced. " At the present moment, for example, an important change in tribal organization is gradually spreading through the tribe from north to south. . . . That changes have been introduced—in fact are still being introduced—is a matter of certainty ; the difficulty to be explained is how in face of the rigid conservatism of the native, which may be said to be one of his leading features, such changes can possibly even be mooted." They come to the conclusion that " if one or two of the most powerful men settled upon the advisability of intro-

[1] Weeks, " J. R. A. I.," XXXIX, 108.
[2] Spencer and Gillen, " Central Tribes," 11.

ducing some change, even an important one, it would be quite possible for this to be agreed upon and carried out." And they explain the process by means of the frequent local meetings for the performance of their sacred ceremonies, and of the larger meetings for these and other purposes at which men from a wider area attend and take part, and at which any changes locally adopted, and any suggestions for change, would certainly be discussed first by the headmen of local groups, and if they were agreed, finally by the entire tribe. They refer also to the tribal traditions as recognizing changes and attributing them to individuals—changes as great as a change in the method of initiation and in the marriage-laws. The traditions in question are not to be relied on for details : they are ætiological tales ; but they do recognize the fact of change, and that the present laws require explanation and justification.[1]

This hypothesis of the procedure among the Arunta and other tribes of the centre of Australia derives confirmation from what is known of the procedure among some of the aboriginal and hill tribes of India. The Oraons occupying the plateau of Chota Nagpur are an essentially conservative people. But they have yielded from time to time to many civilizing influences, notably in the social organization of the tribe. " Whether the earlier steps in that process were for the most part unconscious or not, there can be hardly any doubt that in its later stages human mind and human effort have played a considerable part. In our own days we find in almost every Oraon village one or two Bhuinhars [descendants of the first settlers who are looked up to with respect and deference by the general

[1] *Ibid.*, 12 *sqq.*

body of the people]—sometimes comparatively younger men—who, though not always the actual village head-men, yet exercise considerable influence over their fellow-villagers by reason of their superior intelligence and personality. Such persons appear capable of introducing a new social usage to supplement or modify older usages. This is probably the way in which a number of social usages of their neighbours, the Hindus, have been gradually grafted on the social and religious systems of the Oraons in many parts of the Oraon country, and this is how in our days certain objection-able practices are being given up." [1]

The Nabaloi Igorot of Luzon were governed by a council of the wisest men. If the natives may be trusted, this council had power even to change the customary law which they administered. This body of customary law was ascribed to the people them-selves " long ago." When a change was decreed, a ceremony of drinking *tapuy*, a fermented drink made from rice, was performed by the council, and the pro-posed change of law was required to be submitted to the people, and agreed to by a majority. The last change, as stated by a native of about sixty years of age, took place when he was a young man. It concerned the punishment of a young man and an unmarried girl who had violated the Nabaloi sexual morals. The sentence for this crime was to forfeit a carabao, a cow, or a pig, which they were condemned to kill, and which was then eaten by the people. The council decided that these animals were becoming few, and that it would be well to change the law. Accordingly the people gathered together and the majority approved the

[1] Roy, " Oraons," 433.

decision of the council. The exact effect of the change however is not stated. It seems too that every settlement had a separate and independent council ; so probably the council and people of one settlement were not bound by the decisions of another.[1]

The procedure of the Nabaloi Igorot on at least as high a stage as the Oraon, and much higher than that of the Australian Blackfellows, is similar, as far as it goes, in originating from the wise elders, and being confirmed by the assembly of the people at large.

Further evidence is furnished by the Bantu tribes in the south-eastern corner of Africa. They have regular laws, though unwritten, which every one from the highest to the lowest is bound to obey, and carrying penalties for disobedience. The repositories of these laws are the chiefs and their councillors, and indeed the whole body of the people, " for as the laws are simple and few, every one is supposed to know them." In some cases a law may be changed, or set aside by the judicial decision of a chief which is accepted and cited as a precedent in much the same way as a " leading case " made by the judges in this country. But the most usual course is that the chief first consults with his councillors over any alteration or addition to the laws that may be suggested. He then calls a meeting of the tribe when it is fully discussed and finally decided one way or the other. The chief has, of course, considerable influence ; but " the people have both directly and indirectly a part in framing these laws." That changes are not very frequent " is illustrated by the fact that, among the Kafir and Basuto tribes, the fundamental

[1] " Univ. Cal. Pub.," XV, 237.

laws are similar, though there may be slight modifica-
tions in immaterial points." But the point is that
they do take place, that they emanate from individual
suggestion, and that they are brought before an assembly
of the tribe for debate and decision.[1]

The similarity of this procedure to that hypotheti-
cally formulated by Spencer and Gillen for the Australian
tribes—but formulated, it must be remembered, after
long and careful and sympathetic observation of the
natives—is the more striking, inasmuch as the Kafir
tribes of Africa stand on a different plane of culture
from the Arunta, a much higher plane from every
point of view. If we turn to North America, where
the culture of the native tribes is certainly very different
from both, though perhaps not on the whole higher
than that of the Kafirs, we find among the Osages and
Omaha, whose traditions and institutions have been
minutely studied in recent years by Miss Alice Fletcher
and Mr. Francis La Flesche, himself the son of an
Indian chief, definite traditions of legislation. These
two related Siouan tribes now located, the former in
the State of Missouri, the latter in the State of Nebraska,
are not in their original habitat. They have reached
their present homes by various migrations from the east
of the Mississippi, and both have undergone many
vicissitudes which have left decisive marks on their
institutions. Of this they are fully aware, and their
sacred legends recount the various steps by which
their laws and organizations have developed. The
record of the Omaha is thus summed up by the authors
referred to : " Every acquisition that bettered the
condition of the people was the result of the exercise

[1] " Cape Nat. Laws Com.," Evid., 475 ; App., 43, 58.

of the mind. ' And the people thought ' is the preamble to every change ; every new acquirement, every arrangement devised to foster tribal unity and to promote tribal strength, was the outcome of thought. The regulation of the annual tribal hunt, wherein the individual was forced to give way for the good of the whole people ; the punishment of murder as a social offence ; the efforts to curb the disintegrating war-spirit, to bring it under control, to make it conserve rather than disrupt the unity of the tribe—all were the result of ' thought.' So too was the tribal organization itself, which was based on certain ideas evolved from thinking over natural processes that were ever before their observation. The Sacred Legend speaks truly when it says : ' And the people thought.' " [1] The Sacred Legend of the Osages relates four distinct stages in the development of the governmental organization of the tribe, from the time when " the affairs of the people were in a continual state of chaos and confusion, and there were no fixed rules of action," down to the completion of the organization, as it now is, or until lately continued.[2]

The sacred legends cannot of course be accepted as literal narratives of fact. They have doubtless assumed their present form in comparatively recent times long after most of the events which they relate can have happened. But they do represent the tribal beliefs, and the tribal consciousness that the laws and institutions are far from primitive ; they embody the admission that there has been change and progress throughout the tribal history. Naturally, among a democratic

[1] " R. B. E.," XXVII, 608.
[2] " Smith's Misc. Collections," LXX, 110.

people they lay no stress on the individual initiation of the reforms, attributing them all to the action of the community, to which finally they are in fact due.

Usually it is probable that novelties are introduced by the clash of two or more peoples. Then the change may be effected by the subjugation of one people by the other, as happened in the conquest of the autochthonous inhabitants of Peru by the Incas. This has constantly been the result of the occupation of the territories of barbarous and savage tribes by a European power, in which a softening of ancient and brutal customs has been forced upon the population subjugated. Or it may be effected by the settlement in the midst of one people by another people who ultimately merge in the original population. This is what seems to have taken place in the Melanesian islands, in which Dr. Rivers has discovered traces of at least three strata of institutions. Such a conclusion is only to be arrived at by a very careful and minute analysis of the resulting culture. Still more obscure is the case where changes have occurred by the mere contact of peoples, without conquest or any appreciable or permanent settlement or intermingling. They may have been adopted by one people voluntarily imitating another, or being driven to new arrangements in order more effectually to organize for the purpose of meeting the competition or hostilities set up by the contact. This cause is doubtless answerable for many changes in every human relation, as it undoubtedly is for the introduction into different communities of a number of material fabrics and processes, which have spread inventions and discoveries into the remotest corners of the world. On the other hand, it may be that customs and institutions have been changed or abandoned in the course of migration, or by the alteration of climate, such as is known to have occurred repeatedly in various countries. Migration or an alteration of climate would rapidly or slowly effect a change of environment to which more archaic customs and institutions might be inappropriate, perhaps even injurious or impossible. To this cause has been attributed the abandonment by the ancestors of the Polar Eskimo of reindeer-hunting and salmon-fishing, which it is probable they used at one time to practise. If they did, the tribal memory no longer preserves the record. And this must have happened repeatedly among people everywhere : the change which we infer has taken place in the midst of a people with no means, other than oral tradition, of recording it, and the oral tradition in which it was for a time embedded has perished in the competition with other more recent, more dramatic, and more exciting memories.

Where from whatever cause, save perhaps alien conquest and compulsion, a people has adopted new laws and institutions, or even new objects of material culture, the influence of important personages has always been weighty, if not decisive, as attested in the case of the Australian and South African tribes. Although the traditions of the Omaha and the Osages do not refer to this influence, it must, from what we know of North American Indian practices and susceptibility to eloquence, have been as signally powerful among them. Indeed, we need not go further than our own countrymen in these modern days to recognize the effect of the advocacy of a point of national policy

or a change of law by a trusted leader of energy, eloquence, and proved resource. But in all these cases
the change is in the long run dependent upon acceptance
by the whole community; and the influence of individuals, however highly placed or however trusted,
is confined to their sagacity in perceiving and thinking
out what changes are necessary or desirable, and to
their skill in persuading their fellows of their sincerity
in exemplifying the changes they advocate. Rarely,
perhaps never, does this influence rise to the height of
that attributed to the more or less mythical Lycurgus,
by which the entire constitution of Sparta was revolutionized or created.

Religion has generally been a conservative, not an
innovating, force. Yet it is probable that occasionally
at least, it has played its part in introducing and
sanctioning legislation. The influence of the shaman,
or medicine-man, is by no means negligible in the lower
strata of civilization; and there can be no doubt that
it has from time to time been called in aid of changes
in the laws. Without the co-operation of the medicine-
man, changes would again and again have been impossible. More than once the oracles of ancient Greece
threw their weight on the side of innovation.[1]

When the worship of definite personal gods had
developed, their authority was frequently invoked
by the law-giver for his legislation. The Mosaic law
in its present shape exhibits more than one change
made during considerable intervals of time. It is all
ascribed to Jahweh. Mohammed, legislating for the
Arabs, claimed to do so by the immediate command
of Allah, and imposed his code in the long run on

[1] See, for example, Herod, I, 65; II, 52; IV, 161.

peoples whom he did not contemplate, and of whose very existence he was ignorant. Zoroaster, the Persian, by a similar device, long before him effected a similar and equally lasting, though not equally widespread, result. Hammurabi legislated for Babylonia in the name of Shamash. Minos, the legendary King of Crete, is said to have received his laws from his father Zeus. At Rome the fabulous legislation of Numa was dictated by the nymph Egeria and the other divine ladies, whose amiable society the king enjoyed from time to time. More authentic is the record of King Alfred the Great. At the head of his code, formed by collecting, collating, and choosing, or rejecting, with the advice of his witan, the laws of his predecessors in Wessex, Kent, and Mercia, and by adding new laws where he deemed necessary, he prefixes the Hebrew decalogue and other divine laws, including from the New Testament the authoritive letter from the Church of Jerusalem, contained in the fifteenth chapter of the Acts of the Apostles, and addressed to the Gentile converts. The intention is clear by these devices to ensure the acceptance and permanent adoption of a code thus invested with the sanctity of religion.

This purpose has no doubt been facilitated by the indistinction before alluded to as characteristic of the institutions of the lower culture. The savage mind more readily synthesizes than analyses, more easily seizes the points of agreement, the likenesses between two or more objects, than their differences. For the savage, and a long way up into civilization, the policy of a tribe is one and indivisible. Every part of it is equally authoritative, because it is equally handed down from antiquity. It is only we, observing and reasoning from the standpoint of civilization, who analyse its institutions under various heads—law, medicine, religion, magic, social observances, and so forth. We may distinguish between different kinds or subjects of law ; we may sever religion from magic, and magic from medicine ; the members of the community draw no such distinctions. Such analysis is not possible to them. They see nothing grotesque or incongruous in publishing in the name of God a code combining ritual, moral, agricultural, and medical with what we understand as strictly juridical prescriptions, prohibitions of homicide, rape, theft, and fraud, with meticulous directions as to food—what must be avoided, what may be eaten, and when, and how, it must be prepared—the treatment of disease, the method of tillage, the garb and ceremonies of mourning for the dead. The same code in the same Divine Name, and with equal authority, may make regulations for the conduct of commercial transactions and of the most intimate conjugal relations, as well as for a complex and splendid ceremonial of divine worship. All these are part of the national institutions, equally carrying the sense of obligation, and all actively fostering the sense of solidarity ; therefore no impropriety can be felt in ascribing them to the same source.

When we look critically at such a code it becomes obvious that the core of the legislation is a series of taboos of a more or less primitive character which have persisted into a higher stratum of culture. It has been plausibly suggested that law originates from taboos. This would account for the fact that almost all early codes consist of prohibitions. It is as if the law-giver were preoccupied by the attempt to prevent the people from going astray rather than by the effort to guide them aright. But it must be observed that the taboos appearing thus in a code are for the most part concerned with ritual prescriptions, which are thus found embedded in a body of laws of a more social and ethical character. Such a code in fact, is a collection of the ancient customs of the community, diverse in origin, and already gradually and imperceptibly modified from time to time, together with the law-giver's conscious amendments. Religion, as is natural in a code attributed to a divine origin, occupies a considerable share of the bulk, whether we reckon it quantitatively, or qualitatively ; and religion at this stage has not by any means freed itself from its primeval connexion with magic. But the whole of a primitive people's customs do not deal with the supernatural. In fact, religion and morals are unthinkable apart from the social state ; and the social organization therefore is the beginning of law. The religious organization expressed in negative and positive commands is not the origin of law but a development, though an early development, and one which is constantly striving to overshadow the rest.

On the other hand, so close is the association between law and morals that they are in the early stages with difficulty distinguished. The earliest human aggregation, which we may call a horde, or an organized community, lies so far back in the ages, and is so distant from us, not only in time, but in culture, that its very existence is only a speculation, and of its circumstances and form we have no evidence whatever. But we may surmise that its constituent members, little above the brutes as they may have been, must have regulated their conduct towards one another by some rules.

These rules were possibly derived from their pre-human experience (compare the conduct of cattle, deer, and flocks of birds), and may have been only half-conscious. They must however have sufficed to keep the peace within the horde, and constituted a body of ethics appropriate to that stage. Law and morals were identical. They could not remain identical long. A human society, however slowly progressive, which does progress, carries with it a progressive ethic. That ethic is the result of experience, and of a constantly widening sympathy; and it outruns the tardier steps of custom and definite law. Its existence apart from law may remain long unrevealed. But amid the countless experiences of human nature sooner or later it clashes with the general custom, and men become aware of the unsuspected gulf between law and moral feeling. Nursing an ideal unknown to law, it becomes one of the chief agents in the gradual changes undergone by the law. Its existence is established as distinct from, and reaching beyond, law; and in its activities, in spite of all conservatism, lies the hope of the advance of civilization.

INDEX

Abipones, 117
Adoption into tribe, 35, 36
Adultery, 61, 63, 144, 146, 158,
   165, 166, 173
Africa, African, 49, 62, 65, 112,
   145, 146, 160, 188, 189,
   192, 208
   Central, 50, 76, 125
   French West, 115
   South, 76, 192, 211
   West, 7, 50, 77, 115, 124,
   156–159, 160, 182, 190, 200
Agui, 156–158
Amazons, 41
   Upper, 51, 97
America, 48, 115
   North, 36, 70, 76, 78, 112, 122,
   125, 126, 131, 136, 160, 166,
   208
   North American Indian, 211
   North-West, 160
   South, 89
Ancestor worship, 32, 33
Andaman Islands, 12–15
Angámi, 110–111
Anglo-Saxon law, 43, 161, 192,
   193
Anyanja, 61, 166
Arabs, Arabia, 62, 70, 121, 212
Arunta, 7, 17, 62, 77, 141, 143,
   163, 205
Asage, 36
Assam, 83
Australia, Australian, 15–17,
   18, 20, 21, 27, 31, 48, 49,
   50, 67, 76, 77, 78, 93, 121,
   124, 141, 146, 204, 208, 211
   Blackfellows, 6, 20, 74, 76, 77,
   78, 79, 86, 163, 164, 171,
   204, 207

Australia, Australian—contd.
   Central, 53, 77, 78, 205
   South, 126, 127
Aztecs, 35, 37–39

Babylonia, 213
Baganda, 49, 119
Ba-ila, 150, 151, 180, 181
   buditazhi, 180, 181
Balearic islanders, 62
Bangala, 104, 105, 203
Banks' Islands, 30, 31
Bantu, 6 (note 1), 55, 61, 66, 74,
   76, 77, 78, 83, 104, 105, 106,
   114, 118, 159, 165, 176, 177,
   192, 207.
Ba-Ronga, 103, 104
Bechuana, 49, 202
Berber, 83
Betrothal customs, 65
Blood :
   avenger of, 58
   covenant, 36, 131–135
   feud, 53–55, 58–59
   money, or *wergild*, 154, 155,
   197, 198
   spilling of, 171
Bororó, 139
Borough English, 111
Bougainville, island of, 130
Boumali, 131, 132
Bride-price or *jujur*, 169
Brides, customs concerning, 62,
   64, 66, 68, 69, 71, 74, 114
Brittany, 90
Buandik, 88, 89
Bukana, 131
Bulgaria, 152
Bushongo, 198, 199

217